THE POWER OF POEMS

Teaching the Joy of Writing Poetry

Margriet Ruurs

MAUPIN
HOUSE

The Power of Poems
Teaching the Joy of Writing Poetry

Cover Design: *Maria Messenger*
Book Design: *Billie Hermansen*

Library of Congress Cataloging-in-Publication Data

Ruurs, Margriet.
   The power of poems : teaching the joy of poetry / Margriet Ruurs.
     p. cm.
   Includes bibliographical references and index.
   ISBN 0-929895-44-4
     1. Poetry--Study and teaching (Elementary) 2. Poetry--Authorship--
Study and teaching (Elementary)--Activity programs. I. Title.

   LB1575 .R88 2000
   372.64--dc21

Margriet Ruurs is available to speak at conferences and to visit schools,
libraries and art centers for author talks and professional development
workshops throughout North America. Reach her at ruurs@junction.net, or
through Maupin House.

Other Books by Margriet Ruurs:

Virtual Maniac: Silly and Serious Poems for Kids
A Mountain Alphabet
Emma and the Coyote
Emma's Eggs
On the Write Track
Spectacular Spiders
When We Go Camping
Big Little Dog

Maupin House, Inc.
PO Box 90148, Gainesville, FL 32607
1-800-524-0634, Fax: 352-373-5546, info@maupinhouse.com
www.maupinhouse.com

Publishing Professional Resources that Improve Classroom Performance

To Anne Wilson, Kate and Sue
who gave me roots and wings as a writer.

Teacher

If stories grew in gardens,
a gardener you'd be.
To tend and grow bouquets
in colorful harmony.

Into a palette of petals
You'd coax each budding plant,
support its climbing vines
with caring, nurturing hand.

You'd water, weed and nourish
each hesitant new flower.
Guide it to brilliant sunlight,
encourage and empower.

But gardens soon will wither
when summer days turn cool
and children grow from reading
and what they learn in school.

So you encourage readers
to use their magic powers
to tend the gardens of the world
and grow more brilliant flowers.

*Special Thanks
to Diana Wilkes,
for the constructive criticism,
and to Kees,
for putting up with me
while writing this book.*

Contents

CHAPTER 1

Poetry Philosophy

As a writer of children's books, I am invited into classrooms
all across North America. Because I love to perform my own
poetry, I am often asked to conduct poetry-writing workshops with
kids of all ages. I find that poetry is a wonderful resource: lyrical
language and rhythmic patterns provide opportunities for reading
out loud in the classroom, for memorization and choral speaking, as
well as for independent reading and writing.

What is Poetry?

The dictionary says, "Poetry is. . . a composition produced by
creative imagination." How exciting to be able to allow your
students to use their creative imagination to compose a piece of
writing *and* help them learn at the same time! Because a poem is a
story delivered in a rhythmical format, children who write poetry
learn to express their creativity, develop and refine several skills,
and, in the process, have fun.

Poetry is a celebration of language, a play with words. It is music
for the mind that can help a child to tell a story in a unique way.
Poetry is one of the earliest forms of literature to which children are
exposed, and they love its natural rhythm and rhyme. Through
nursery rhymes, lap games, and songs, children develop language.
No wonder they like it: nursery rhymes, folktales, and ballads are
some of the most pleasant, and earliest, forms of story telling.

These forms of poetry, through rich language, were used to teach morals and values as they entertained. Some nursery rhymes are, in fact, riddles. What a joy, not only to enjoy the sounds of the rhyme but to discover the power in coming to understand the riddle and the secret message within it.

Too many students have been exposed to a narrow range of poetry. Often, especially by the time they hit middle school, they feel that poetry has to be something serious. They do, however, fondly recall nursery rhymes or Dr. Seuss books.

Many students feel that poetry has to rhyme to be poetry. But it doesn't need to rhyme! Poetry can be whimsical. It can also be serious. Poetry is a form of writing usually written in shorter sentences than prose. The whole poem can be taken to heart and interpreted by each individual.

Poems can bring strong visual images to mind while speaking to the emotions. They help us to look at the world differently, to see something through different eyes. Recently I read an anecdote in "Reader's Digest." A mother who never used makeup had a make-over done. Her five year old looked at her face and exclaimed, "Mom! You look like a sunset!" *That* is poetry!

Why Poetry?

Because poetry can be so satisfying and support a wide range of learning. Because the rhythm of poetry comes naturally to children. Because the potential of poetry lies within the minds of all children. We need to nurture it with an abundance of words and then hand them the skills to refine and polish their poems.

Because the use of poetic language in the classroom brings along a certain energy, a joy that is hard to capture in prose. Stories can be spellbinding, but poems have a special sort of magic that naturally appeals to kids and therefore makes it easy to introduce young students to reading and writing by means of poetry. Writing poetry opens up a way of expressing oneself and allows the student to see the world through different eyes. A poem says something in a neat, different package.

How to Use This Book

When I started writing this book, it was my intent to help you teach the *writing* of poems to children. I soon realized that we can't separate the writing from *reading* lots and lots of poems. So you will find in this book ways to start kids writing and reading poetry.

I suggest you read the entire book first, for your own information as well as to understand fully the structure of the activities. The book addresses the components to writing poetry:

The content: *What* are you writing about? Will your poem deal with an observation or a thought, a feeling, or perhaps it will tell a funny story? Will it have a message or simply be there to have fun with the words? Where *do* you get ideas?

and **The craft**: *How* do you form the words into a poem? What tricks of the trade are there? How can you make use of sounds and rhythms to help shape your poem?

I don't think you can look at one independently of the other. Each builds on the other. You need to know what you want to write about, and learning more about the techniques of poetry helps you to do so more effectively. But what if you knew all of the techniques and had no idea what to write about? So, in this book we will look at both aspects. Look for the icon that indicates whether each activity deals with **craft** or **content** .

You can adapt this entire book easily to whichever grade level you teach by using different poetry books for younger or older kids. I have aimed the activities at grades 3 to 8, but you can use them with your second graders or ninth graders just as well by adapting the books and poems you use as examples. The main bibliography, at the end of this book, is in alphabetical order by author, and I have indicated which titles are suited for younger and older audiences. I have also added a bibliography at the end of each chapter, with books listed in alphabetical order by titles. I hope that this makes it easier for you to find a title quickly.

The book will take you through the following steps:

- a look at how poetry will help your students and how it fits the curriculum;
- the prewriting process: the tools you and your students need before the actual writing begins;

- generating ideas to create contents: what to write about, where to get ideas;
- practical writing activities to learn the techniques as well as expand the content;
- editing poems: learning the steps of refining the rough poem;
- publishing/sharing poems: the ultimate goal of writing a great poem!

I'll begin by offering you suggestions for creating a poetry class-room, generating ideas, and beginning the prewriting process. The writing activities in Chapter 3 allow you to share different ways of creating poetry with your students. The activities are based on producing content as well as on building technical skills. They are tried and true ways of writing that I have found to work well to get kids committed, and they are aimed at helping you to discover the enjoyment and excitement of using poetry in the classroom on a daily basis. The order in which the writing activities are presented allows students' writing skills to grow throughout the process. **I recommend that you use Prewriting Activities 1-3 and Writing Activities 4 and 5 in that order.** The activities that follow these first foundation activities can be used whenever they suit your schedule.

Chapter 4 will help you and your students to critique and edit the poems. In Chapter 5 are suggestions to publish and share your students' poetry, both in print and on the Internet.

How Do We Encourage the Writing of Poetry?

As teachers, we have an obligation to let children experience the *joy* of reading and writing poetry. To do that successfully, the child has to be *motivated* to write. To truly motivate a child to be a writer, we need to do more than teach specific skills. When I was a child, I used to hate having to analyze poetry. I didn't *want* to explain *why* I liked a particular sentence or guess at what the author had meant when he or she wrote that line. I just wanted to enjoy the poem for what it was. I wanted to savor the sounds, the rhythm, and maybe try writing my own poems.

There is much more to teaching poetry to children than teaching specific skills or having them "dissect" poems. When students visit a museum they're not allowed to scratch at the varnish of a painting or turn the canvas over to see what's underneath: they observe and absorb the complete piece as a work of art, taking it to mind as a whole.

Let's treat poetry the same way. Let's enjoy and savor the words. It's okay not to like a certain poem or to love another one. We can't all like the same thing. But let's submerge our kids in poems. Once they have built up a vocabulary and mastered some of the poetry-writing techniques, then we can take a closer look at different structures of poems.

As a writer, I don't believe that writers write poetry to have a reader guess at what they might have meant. A writer creates with imagination so that a reader can make the poem his or hers and savor it for what it means to him or her. Teachers must be careful not to impose on the children their own views of what the poem means. Let the children take the poem to heart and interpret it for themselves. Sometimes poems are pieces of writing just to be savored.

When first embarking upon a poetry course, students sometimes confess that they don't really *like* poetry. What a great challenge to prove to them that poetry need not be boring! Let's take that challenge and find ways of writing poetry that appeal to the students and that allow them to *play* with words! The learning will follow.

Remember how nice it felt to squeeze Play Dough between your fingers and to make whatever shapes came to mind? Maybe we should treat language like Play Dough when we write poetry. When we use our imaginations and play with words, it's exciting to see the shape of the poem that emerges.

Special Needs

While all students benefit from poetry, the ESL student, new to the English language, can become familiar with its rhythms and sounds through poetry. No matter what the age of the student, poetry can help familiarize him or her with the sounds of our language. Many advanced picture books are written in rhyme and are suitable for middle and high school students, including:

- *There Were Monkeys in my Kitchen*, by Sheree Fitch.
- *Aska's Animals*, by Warabé Aska and David Day.
- *Animalia*, by Graeme Base.

For younger ESL kids, simple nursery rhymes and games will help ease the tension of learning a new language, for example:

- *The Candlewick Book of First Rhymes.*
- *Bear in Mind, A Book of Bear Poems,* by Bobbye S. Goldstein.
- *More Surprises,* An I Can Read Book, by Lee Bennett Hopkins.

Students with learning disabilities can often produce poetry with a tape recorder or word processor. Dictation works wonderfully with those students who haven't quite mastered writing skills and who become impatient when they can't write down their thoughts fast enough on paper.

I once worked with a severely physically and mentally disabled student. She wrote poetry and sent it to me via e-mail. I read and critiqued her poems and she responded by editing and rewriting. Her love for language showed itself in her writing. I had no idea that she was disabled until her teacher told me. The use of a computer allowed her to participate in writing to her full capacity. Her teacher added that she had never been so committed, so enthusiastic about anything.

Time to Write

Once you embark on your journey of poetry, you will need to make time. If you have never taught poetry in your classroom, start by reading a poem a day. Use one in language arts; the next day, use one during math. Slowly increase the number of poems you use. Once you are ready to have students write their own poetry, set aside at least half an hour a day. When your students really get into the writing, and when you plan to classroom-publish books of poetry, allow at least an hour a day.

Oh, and One More Thing. . .

While looking at all the ways in which to write, and at all the ways in which to introduce poetry to kids, let's not forget to simply have fun with the process! Having fun writing, having fun picking a subject, having fun sharing and reading out loud will make everything else easier. After all, when you're having *fun*, writing poetry will simply be a breeze!

You may notice that, in this book about poetry, I won't dwell on the forms of haiku or limerick. The reason is simple: I don't like having to count while being creative. Another rule I have while writing poetry is, don't think too much. Just write, have fun with words, and enjoy what you are creating! I have seen this rule to be very liberating for students. Try it in your classroom!

While engaged in meaningful writing, children need to *enjoy* the process if we hope to turn them into lifelong writers. If it isn't fun, how can you get *excited* about it? Making up stories and playing with language can be just that—pure fun. Most writers write because it is what they love to do most. Heaven knows they don't do it for the pay!

However, writing for fun is not frivolous: it plays a role in the long-term development of the craft of writing itself. When it's fun, you'll want to keep practicing it. Within the fun are power and purpose.

The joy of writing poetry can be contagious if it is an engaging and rewarding experience. Writing is an important part of real learning. The use of "real language" implies an authentic meaning: language used by real people for a variety of real purposes and real consequences. When we share our love of reading and writing with children, we should, therefore, use real language and real books, as opposed to basal readers. We should also let them write authentic stories. Using drill sheets or fill-in-the-blank type of activities may help to teach a child the rules of sentence structure or grammar but cannot, and never will, get that child *excited* about writing.

After discussing how to teach your students to write poems, we will look at how your students can share their poetry because, without a real audience to address, what's the use of writing? If I didn't hope that you would be reading this someday, why would I bother putting all this down on paper? I write in hopes of sharing ideas and suggestions with you, in hopes of working together so that we may stimulate children to discover the joy that writing can bring.

Joy doesn't come from filling in the blanks. Joy comes from someone's response to your writing, from seeing someone else laugh or cry when they read your words! Wow! That's powerful stuff.

Poetry and the Language Arts Standards

The activities in this book pertain directly to the skills targeted by state and provincial language arts standards for grades 3-8. Please check your own state or provincial requirements to see how each activity meets specific standards.

U.S. National Language Arts standards expect students to learn to think critically, solve problems, communicate clearly, and be able to learn and work both independently and with others. Students are expected to employ a wide range of strategies as they write and to use different writing process elements appropriately to communicate with disparate audiences for a variety of purposes. The writing activities in this book contribute to this outcome by providing a framework to help students:

- develop reading and writing skills;
- present and respond to ideas, feelings, and knowledge sensitively and creatively;
- use poetry as a way of developing personal values, understanding multicultural heritage, and broadening experience;
- use language confidently to understand and respond thoughtfully to factual and imaginative communications in speech, print, and the media;
- express themselves powerfully and gracefully for a variety of personal and social purposes;
- use language appropriate to the audience and purpose and become comfortable with format of poetry.

Here are some English K-12 National Standards (United States) that are met by the activities in this book:

Reading for Perspective

Students read a wide range of print and nonprint texts to build an understanding of texts, of themselves, and of the cultures of the United States and the world; to acquire new information; to respond to the needs of personal fulfillment.

Evaluating Data

Students conduct research on issues and interests by generating ideas and questions, and by posing problems. They gather, evaluate, and synthesize data from a variety of sources (e.g., print and nonprint texts, artifacts, people) to communicate their discoveries in ways that suit their purpose and audience.

Multicultural Understanding

Students develop an understanding of and respect for diversity in language use, patterns, and dialects across cultures, ethnic groups, geographic regions, and social roles.

Communication Strategies

Students employ a wide range of strategies as they write and use different writing process elements appropriately to communicate with different audiences for a variety of purposes.

Canada does not have national standards. However, each province has its own guidelines and targets. Here are examples from British Columbia's Ministry of Education that are met through the activities in this book:

Prescribed Learning Outcomes, Comprehend and Respond

It is expected that students will identify connections between their own ideas, experiences, and knowledge and a variety of literature. It is expected that students will:

- demonstrate a willingness to choose challenging materials for reading, viewing, or listening for a variety of purposes
- explain their preferences for specific types of literary and informational works
- make explicit connections among central ideas in works that they have read, viewed, or heard
- describe how particular works or literary features evoke personal images, memories, and responses

Prescribed Learning Outcomes, Communicate Ideas and Information

It is expected that students will enhance the precision, clarity, and artistry of their communications by using processes that professional authors and presenters use to appraise and improve their communications. It is expected that students will:

- appraise their own and others' work
- revise and edit their own and others' work for content and clarity
- edit to correct their own and others' use of grammar, spelling, and punctuation using both electronic and manual means

Prescribed Learning Outcomes, Working Together, Grade 4

It is expected that students will use language to interact and collaborate with others to explore ideas and accomplish goals. It is expected that students will:

- assume a variety of roles when interacting in groups
- use the language of praise and constructive feedback when working with others
- listen to and express interest in the ideas of others
- assess their own communications and their contributions to the group

Prescribed Learning Outcomes, Language Arts, Grade 5

It is expected that students will demonstrate their understanding of and abilities to use a variety of forms and styles of communication that are relevant to specific purposes and audiences. It is expected that students will:

- demonstrate pride and satisfaction in using language to create and express thoughts, ideas, and feelings in a variety of oral, written, and electronic forms
- create a variety of personal and informational communications, including written and oral stories, poems, or lyrics; explanations and descriptions; informal oral reports and dramatics;
- apply the basic rules and conventions of writing or speaking for the oral, visual, and written forms they select

Prescribed Learning Outcomes, Language Arts, Grade 5

It is expected that students will use language to explore thoughts, ideas, feelings, and experiences to prepare for their roles in the world. It is expected that students will:

- demonstrate an awareness of how to use language to develop and maintain friendships and relationships in school and in the community
- develop personal communication goals and plans
- demonstrate confidence in their abilities to communicate effectively in various classroom situations

Prescribed Learning Outcomes, Comprehension, Grade 4

It is expected that students will draw reasoned conclusions from information found in various written, spoken, or visual communications and defend their conclusions rationally. It is expected that students will:

- identify common literary elements in various genres
- compare their responses to several selections

Prescribed Learning Outcomes, Language Arts, Grade 4

It is expected that students will demonstrate their understanding of written, oral, and visual communications. It is expected that students will:

- describe and recount key ideas or information from various media
- interpret their impressions of simple and direct stories, poetry, other print material, and electronic media
- organize information or ideas they have read, heard, or viewed in the form of simple charts, webs, or illustrations
- locate specific details in stories, poems, mass media, and audio-visual media
- identify the main information given in illustrations, maps, or charts
- demonstrate an awareness of relationships among the elements of story structure, including plot, setting, and characters

Whether you have already written much poetry or whether you have *never* tackled it, this book will support you in letting poetry flow throughout your curriculum for the sheer pleasure of sharing. I will make suggestions for doing this by helping you to throw a poetry party during socials, to use poetry to inspire your art curriculum, to point out the lyrics of a song during music lessons, and to add some rhythm to math! Then poetry will truly come alive in your classroom!

Books to Support a Poetry-Rich Environment

Booth, David. *Classroom Voices*. Canada: Harcourt Brace, 1994.

Booth, David. *Literacy Techniques*. Pembroke, 1996.

Booth, David, with Bill Moore. *Poems Please*. Pembroke, 1988.

Buzzeo, Toni, with Jane Kurtz. *Terrific Connections with Authors, Illustrators and Storytellers: Real Space and Virtual Links*. Libraries Unlimited, 1999.

Close, Susan, with Faye Brownlie and Linda Wingren. *Reaching for Higher Thought, Reading Writing Thinking Strategies*. Arnold, 1988.

Close, Susan. *Tomorrow's Classroom Today, Strategies for Creating Active Readers, Writers and Thinkers*. Pembroke, 1990.

Esbensen, Barbara Juster. *A Celebration of Bees, Helping Children to Write Poetry*. New York: Henry Holt. Can only be ordered from: tory@ttinet.com or 612-929-2065.

Fox, Mem. *Radical Reflections: Passionate Opinions on Teaching, Learning and Living*. Harcourt, Brace, 1993.

Freeman, Marcia S. *Building a Writing Community*. Gainesville, FL: Maupin House, 1995, 1997.

Goforth, Frances S. *Literature & The Learner*. New York: Wadsworth, 1998.

Jobe, Ron, with Mary Dayton-Sakari. *Reluctant Readers*. Pembroke, 1999.

Jobe, Ron, with Paula Hart. *Canadian Connections*. Pembroke, 1991.

McCormick Calkins, Lucy. *Lessons from a Child: On the Teaching and Learning of Writing*. Heinemann, 1983.

Moore, William H. *Words That Taste Good*. Pembroke.

Nodelman, Perry. *The Pleasures of Children's Literature*. Longman, 1992.

Spink, John. *Children as Readers*. London: Clive Bingley, 1989.

Chapter 1 Bibliography and Web Sites

Bibiliography

Animalia, by Graeme Base. Willowisp Press, 1986.

Aska's Animals, by Warabé Aska and David Day. Garden City, N.Y.: Doubleday, 1991.

Bear in Mind, A Book of Bear Poems, by Bobbye S. Goldstein. New York: Viking Kestrel, 1989.

More Surprises, An I Can Read Book, by Lee Bennett Hopkins. New York, Harper & Row.

The Candlewick Book of First Rhymes. Cambridge, Mass.: Candlewick Press, 1996.

There Were Monkeys in My Kitchen, by Sheree Fitch. Toronto: Doubleday Canada, 1992.

Web Sites

http://www.education-world.com/standards/national/lang_arts/english/k_12.shtml

A listing of national standards for language arts, from the National Council of English Teachers. This site has links to view standards for each state.

CHAPTER 2

Preparing for Poetry

Prerequisites of a Poetry Classroom

Physical Environment

A physical environment conducive to writing poetry is a classroom that is saturated with words. Books, a reading corner, poems on the wall, scrap paper to use when an idea "hits" should all be readily available.

The more you read the better a writer you'll be. Therefore, I recommend that you supply a wide variety of poetry for the students to read and look through. Frances S. Goforth, in *Literature & the Learner*, says, "Saturate children with a variety of poems representing various poetic forms, types and elements."

Here is a sample selection of books of poetry particularly suited to be read out loud. Display as many as you can find of these and other favorite titles.

- *Rainbows, Head Lice and Pea Green Tile: Poems in the Voice of the Classroom Teacher,* by Brod Bagert.
- *Dinosaurs,* selected by Lee Bennett Hopkins.
- *Scared Silly! A Book for the Brave,* by Marc Brown.
- *Toes in My Nose and Other Poems,* by Sheree Fitch.
- *What's on the Menu?* selected by Bobbye S. Goldstein.
- *Poetry Party,* by Bruce Lansky.

- *I Can Read with My Eyes Shut!* by Dr. Seuss.
- *Alligator Pie,* by Dennis Lee.
- *Barn Dance,* by Bill Martin Jr. and John Archambault.
- *Something Big Has Been Here,* by Jack Prelutsky.

Reading aloud from books of poetry will help students extend their vocabulary while hearing the structure of sentences, the meter of the poem, and the use of techniques, such as metaphor or alliteration.

See the bibliography at the end of this chapter for more books particularly suited for reading out loud.

Even, or perhaps I should say, particularly, if you teach upper middle school, supply your students with Shakespeare as well as with Dr. Seuss, Bill Pete, and Roald Dahl. Once, when I served as chair of our local school board, I was asked to address the graduating class of our high school. Rather than composing a boring speech, I chose to read them *Oh, the Places You'll Go,* by Dr. Seuss. His eloquent words evoked both laughter and tears. No one could have talked about the sentiments for such an occasion better. Years later, at a supermarket checkout, the clerk told me she was in that graduating class and how much they all had loved hearing that poem!

A book that is not a book of poetry but you might want to include in your display is *Oh, the Places He Went,* by Maryann N. Weidt. This biography of Dr. Seuss will interest anyone who likes his writing. Books of poetry as well as books about poets are valuable resources to inspire new writers. Another delicious book about poetry to read aloud is *The Bat Poet,* by Randall Jarrell.

The physical environment also should offer students a comfortable writing space. That can be at their desk, but it may also be on the floor or in a corner. Before allowing my students this choice, I have made the rule clear: "You can sit anywhere you like as long as you write hard." They know that if they don't concentrate on their writing they lose the privilege of choosing a workspace. If you decide to allow students to write where they find themselves most comfortable, be sure to hold them responsible for their behavior.

As I mentioned in the previous chapter, allow sufficient time in your daily schedule to write. Increase the amount of time as your students become more skilled. They will start to ask for more time as their enjoyment of the writing increases.

Keep on hand a supply of scrap paper, lined paper, and pencils for when *that great idea* strikes!

Freedom of Choice

Let's look at some necessary ingredients for successful poetry writing. Choice of *topic* is important in motivating kids to read as well as to write. When you go to the library you have a wealth of choices available. No one tells you which book you must read. You choose according to your own personal tastes and interests. Perhaps you pick a specific genre or a topic about which you want to learn more. Perhaps you choose your favorite author. But the *choice* is yours.

Exposing students to a wide variety of topics, genres, and authors gives them an opportunity to develop their own preferences. Even if the choice is limited to the number of books in your classroom, the student makes his or her own choice and will be more committed to reading the book than if it were assigned without options.

The same holds true for writing. When kids are free to choose their own topics, even if given a limited range of topics from which to choose, they will be more committed to the writing process. If you told me to write about, say, dinosaurs, I would have a hard time becoming committed because I'm not particularly interested in dinosaurs. But if you gave me a *choice*, I might research and write about. . . ladybugs! I might just be "into" ladybugs right now. I could find out why they are called ladybugs, what purpose they serve in nature, or even write a ladybug poem! Next month I might want to write about blizzards or mountain climbing. . .

Parents have sometimes asked me if they should be concerned because their child was only interested in one particular topic and wouldn't write about anything else. Poems about race cars, stories about race cars, nonfiction about race cars. I believe we should applaud that kind of intense interest. Feed that interest by giving your students more resources on the topic, more books to read. *Let* them read, let them research, let them write. Jim's interest in race cars may not interest you and it may even last for a whole year, but eventually he'll move on to something else. In the process, he'll acquire crucial skills for reading, researching, and writing.

By grades 8 or 9, many kids are intrigued by the topic of death. I have seen happy, well-balanced kids write very serious poems about death or suicide. Writing might just be the healthy way to deal with such complex issues at that age. Their pieces of writing may even lead to wonderful discussions of the topic, giving you an opportunity to allay fears and to be in tune with your student's concerns.

A Purpose to Write

All authors write for a real purpose, so why not children? If your students have no idea what the purpose of a writing assignment is or if their only purpose is to get a mark, they won't put their heart and soul into it. In these cases their writing won't reflect true feelings nor will it have the quality that it would have if the students have a more meaningful purpose and truly *care* about their writing.

Often the purpose to write a poem will be self-expression. The purpose of creating tongue twisters or silly rhymes can be purely to have fun with language. And, at some point, the purpose in writing another poem will be to complete a book. But mostly, we will look at poems as a way to put thoughts and feelings into a package that is fun to create and that appeals to the reader.

Of course, the more you write the more skilled you become. Writing for practice may be one reason to write, so, if we can package the practice into fun, engaging activities, it will also serve a real purpose for students. When students have a true purpose to write, they show more commitment and the enthusiasm to write more.

The Need for an Audience

All authors write so that someone will read their writing. Students can find meaning in writing by realizing who their audiences are. As teachers or parents, we can demonstrate the joy of reading as we share a genuine interest in the *contents* of a poem.

By reading out loud a text that has captivated us, made us cry, made us laugh, we can show children the true reason for reading and writing. If children realize *why* we read, they will be more motivated to learn *how* to read as well as how to write.

Realizing whom we write for (peers, younger children, adults, etc.) will help the writing. I write very differently when composing a letter to an old friend than when I write a formal thank-you note. An article about teaching is aimed at a different audience than a short story for a children's magazine. Knowing my audience influences my style of writing. Of course, the author may also write just for himself. **Sharing writing with an audience is something we will look at in greater detail in Chapter 5.**

Building Poetic Vocabulary

To write poems, kids need access to a wide variety of words. The more words are available the greater the fun of finding just the right one to go into your sentence. Prepare your students for writing poetry by "wordstorming." **Prewriting Activity 1 in Chapter 3 deals with wordstorming**. It will guide you to select a topic and generate words on that topic, giving your students access to lots of good sounds.

Once they get used to the concept of wordstorming, students can suggest their own topics. Wordstorm often. This activity will increase your students' vocabulary and open their eyes to the possibilities of a poem.

When you make lists of words and ideas on the board, keep a copy on paper for future reference. You could instruct all students to write down the words as you wordstorm, or one student could be assigned to be scribe.

Tools of the Trade

At first, language is the only tool children need to write poems: lots of words to describe their thoughts and feelings—words that enable them to see something in a new light. Poetic language comes naturally to children and many will already be using concepts of which they do not know the technical terms or definitions.

As their poetic vocabulary grows, students can create a wider variety of poems. Learning about the craft options available helps kids grow as poets.

I don't believe that we should throw these writing terms at them until they have "tasted" the joy of writing poems from the heart. I mention the terms here for you, the teacher, but the writing activities for students that focus on these technical skills will come later (**Writing Activity 4 and higher**). Once the students have been introduced to poetry writing and you know that they are ready to learn more, *then* let's gently present them with some techniques.[1]

Rhythm is the beat or meter of a word, a sentence. Rhythm is determined by the number of syllables and spaces in a line and can be used to obtain a certain effect in your poem. You can best hear the rhythm of a poem by reading it out loud. Poets can use short words to make short-sounding sentences or choose long words that fall into a certain rhythm.

Metaphor is a figure of speech that compares two dissimilar things, for example, snowflakes to cottonballs or the ocean to a dragon. Metaphor is a strong tool to use in writing poetry and one that kids often already use unconsciously.

Simile is also a comparison but using the words "like" or "as." "The sky is as black as ink." "Your face looks like the sunset."

Alliteration is the repetition of the same sound. It can include both consonants and vowels (*Emma's Eggs*; a great grizzly). Alliteration is one of the earliest techniques of poetry! This is another strong tool in crafting poetry, but we sometimes need to caution emerging writers not to overuse it!

Personification attributes human characteristics to nonhuman things like animals or objects. (The flowers danced in the field; a grouchy ladybug). A great tool to use when writing poetry, personification allows us to let a bear talk, or a cloud think!

Rhyme is created by using the same sound in the last syllables of a sentence. (cat—fat; dirty—thirty; bicycle—icicle). I hope you noticed that I didn't mention *rhyme* until now. All kids can rhyme but writing a rhyming poem can be very restricting. Often kids think that, in order for it to be a *real* poem, it *has* to rhyme. On the contrary, if the rhyme makes the story line stilted, *don't* rhyme! Here are some examples of common rhyme schemes, all taken from *Virtual Maniac*.

---

[1] For definitions I have referred to the *Harbrace College Handbook*, by John C. Hodges/Mary E. Whitten (HBJ Canada, 1986).

aa bb: A girl named Anna-Belle-Lou
said, "I don't like my hair blonde, I want it blue!"
She painted her hair, not orange or green
but the bluest blue that you've ever seen!

("Anna-Belle-Lou")

ab ab: I *like* making music with my voice
with notes in high and low.
It's such a joyful, cheerful noise
I wonder why my brother hates it so?!

("Singing")

ab ba: Like a bird in the sky
I soar down the slope.
Faster and faster, I hope
I get wings and can fly!

("Downhill")

To stay with this line of thinking—to speak in a metaphor—I will compare writing poetry to carpentry. Give kids a piece of wood and they will turn it into whatever their imagination tells them it is. By the time others can recognize its shape, it is still rough.

We need to take a piece of sandpaper to smooth the shape, to get rid of the splinters, and to make it something that will be kept and treasured. Sometimes a poem will come out perfectly without needing any sanding. But, at other times, applying some of the above-mentioned techniques to the rough shape formed with words will turn the piece of poetry into a treasure as well.

Fitting Poetry into the Daily Schedule

Besides spending time to work specifically on poetry, try to sneak poems into other daily activities. Poetry fits easily into your daily schedule if you use the format to inform, to read, and to write. You can incorporate poetry that informs, as well as excites, into different areas of your curriculum.

Social Studies

Poetry has strong oral roots. Poetry is found throughout history, around the world. Ballads were popular ways of telling stories in the Middle Ages. Many native people use poetry to narrate stories and legends.

Use texts that give information about a period, an event, or places. For instance:

When studying the North, incorporate

- "The Spell of the Yukon," by Robert Service. From: *The Best of Robert Service.*
- *The Cremation of Sam McGee*, by Robert Service.

When studying the environment (pollution),

- *The Sign of the Sea Horse*, by Graeme Base.

To learn place names, use

- "A Wonderful Trip in a Rocketship," by Dennis Lee. From: *The Ice Cream Store.*
- "Kleena Kleene," by Margriet Ruurs. From: *Virtual Maniac.*

Math

Why not lighten up a math problem by reading a math poem?

- "Five Fat Fleas," by Dennis Lee. From: *Jelly Belly.*
- *There Was An Old Woman,* by Steven Kellogg. (Try counting and subtracting the things she eats in this zany book!)
- "Countdown," by Jack Prelutsky. From: *Scared Silly*, selected by Marc Brown.

Try Writing Activity 29 to add some rhyme to reason: poetry to math.

Language Arts

The writing of poetry, of course, fits certain requirements of your language arts curriculum. But books of poetry also can add to the general learning of words, sentence structure, the alphabet, and more, not *just* when you teach poetry. Here are some books you can display in your classroom to use when teaching language arts:

- *Aster Aardvark's Alphabet Adventures,* by Steven Kellogg.

- "The Alphabet from Z to A," by Judith Viorst. From: *With Much Confusion on the Way.*

- "The Grammatical Witch," by Jane Yolen. From: *Best Witches, Poems for Halloween.*

- *The Eleventh Hour,* by Graeme Base (a book full of riddles, missing letters, and puzzles in which kids have to solve a mystery).

- "My Snake," by Jack Prelutsky. From: *Something Big Has Been Here.* (This poem is about a snake who can make the entire alphabet, and it is hilarious. It can be used to perform as well!)

For a variation on the well-known "I Know an Old Woman," try Jean Little's *I Know an Old Laddie. . .* It's full of wonderful rhythm and language play.

If I Had a Paka, by Charlotte Pomerantz, is a book of poems in eleven languages! You learn Swahili, Dutch, Croatian, even Native American words through the well-crafted poems.

Physical Education

There are even poems to use before or after p.e. class!

- "Transformation," by Gordon Korman. From: *The Last Place Sports Poems of Jeremy Bloom.*

- *Hoops,* by Robert Burleigh.

- *Extra Innings, Baseball Poems,* by Lee Bennett Hopkins.

- *Red Dog Blue Fly, Football Poems,* by Sharon Bell Mathis.

Music Curriculum

Writing Activities 8 and 9 focus on poetry as music. These activities are easily adapted to suit your own music curriculum. In addition, you can have students perform or recite poetry from memory while accompanying them on instruments. Have students match instruments to the tone of the poem: gentle bells and triangles for spring rain, a repetitive boom on the tambourine for a giant's footsteps, and so on.

A wonderful book to use with grades 4 and up is *The Worst Band in the Universe,* by Graeme Base. This wild poetic tale deals with musicians and instruments and is accompanied by a CD-ROM.

Also use

- "I Am Growing a Glorious Garden," by Jack Prelutsky.
  From: *Something Big Has Been Here*.

Other Times for Poetry

When assigning homework, have fun by reading a homework poem:

- "Certainly I Did My Homework," by Gordon Korman.
  From: *The D- Poems of Jeremy Bloom*.
- "My Dog Chewed Up My Homework," by Bruce Lansky.
  From: *Poetry Party*.

If your school is undergoing accreditation, read *Hurray for Dieffendoofer Day!* by Dr. Seuss and Jack Prelutsky. Not only will your students love it; it will lift the mood of staff and parents as well.

There are food poems and boot poems, rainy poems and sunny poems, bedtime poems and principal poems. There are poems about bats and frogs and, probably more than any other topic, books of poetry about dinosaurs! You can read a *loud* poem out loud or tape a quiet poem to the door without saying anything. Use enriching poems throughout your day, not just during language arts.

Prewriting Activities

Poems in a Box

To promote the daily use of poems, start a Poetry Box. Use a cardboard box decorated with words and pictures labeled "Poems Please" to stimulate the reading and writing of poems. Give the box a prominent place in the classroom and tell the students that in it you will put some of your favorite poems. Each day you will pull out a poem to read. Invite them to contribute their favorite poems. They can copy a poem from a book or magazine or write their own. You could suggest literary Web sites on the Internet as other sources of finding poems to share. (Be sure to include credit to the author when you read someone else's poem.)

Each day, as you read a poem from the box, students will show more interest. At first you might be the one who reads the daily poem. But soon, your students will be eager to do the reading. Within a short period of time, you may be reading several poems a day. As they gain confidence as writers, the children will contribute more self-written poems. This activity not only encourages students to write, it makes them read more poems.

Making a Picture File

Start looking for funny or interesting pictures in magazines, cut them out, and keep them in a box or file folder. Look specifically for pictures that seem to have a story behind them. What is happening in the picture? What just happened? What will happen next? Who is the main character? Who else is or might be there? What's the story?

Pictures that I have collected include images from:

- pet food commercials:
  - a cat in an Oriental vase
  - a cat licking its lips in a pantry full of food
  - a dog with a bandana, looking very pooped

- ads for carpet cleaners:
  - a gigantic upside-down ice cream cone on a floor
  - little bugs that look like tiny aliens

- and for floor wax:
  - a family and an elephant at the breakfast table.
  - a boy tracking mud all over the house

I have found pictures of dancing carrots, of a beaver lodge with a chimney and a porch, of a girl riding on a polar bear's back, of two men sailing in a shoe.

When you start to look for pictures, you'll discover that many advertisements are very suitable as storytelling pictures. It might take you a little while to find good ones, but I'm sure you'll build a great collection. Keep looking; use very good pictures to eventually replace iffy ones.

Another great place to find good illustrations to generate story ideas: publishers' catalogues. Most book publishers issue a catalogue of new books twice a year. These show book illustrations for new books as well as books on their backlist. Cut out the illustrations and glue them on a sheet of construction paper.

Laminate your picture collection to ensure a longer life. Store them in a manila file folder or large envelope. **I will refer to this picture file in Writing Activity 17.**

Making a Newspaper File

It is often said that truth is more amazing than fiction. Newspaper articles provide some of the best sources for ideas; newspapers are full of amazing happenings. We can use these stories as starting points for creating our own amazing poems. Students can use fictional names, fictional settings, and add as much to the story as they like.

Start looking for and selecting sample stories. These can simply be stories that you like and that you feel you could write more about. There are many funny, touching, or amazing stories in daily papers. Tonight I noticed in my local newspaper two stories that I will cut out:

- chickens stand on guard for our nation, and
- belting bus driver brightens up day, about a bus driver who serenades his passengers all day. What great ideas!

You can also supply your students with a big pile of newspapers and let them find their own poem ideas. If you do that, discuss appropriateness of selected stories—all stories need to be acceptable in a classroom situation. You may even want to mention that you prefer only stories of a humorous or adventurous nature and that you will not approve stories with unacceptable levels of violence as sources for poems.

Mention to students that they may have to search for quite a while before finding a usable story. This activity can encourage them to start reading newspapers and magazines at home to find suitable stories.

Another source for usable news story ideas is the Web site of *USA Today*. This site has a section already marked "Weird News": http://www.usatoday.com/news/nweird.htm

This is a recent article from that site:

Deer Found Taking Bubble Bath

When a couple awoke to strange noises, they thought high winds were rattling their home. What they found was even more unexpected: A deer was taking a bubble bath in their tub. The deer burst through the front door, ran past the couple's bedroom and into the bathroom, somehow managing to turn on the water in the tub and knocking over a bottle of bubble bath. He then submerged himself in the frothy water.

I can definitely see writing a poem about a deer taking a bubble bath!

Keep all suitable newspaper articles in a magnetic photo album for students to use. This protects the paper from yellowing and tearing. Articles I have saved include the following, apparently true, stories. Note how the questions that follow each story help to rough out a poem idea. The article serves as the bones; the questions put meat on the bones! Here are a couple of stories and the kinds of questions to ask.

Kids Find Prehistoric Egg

This article describes how some children were digging in the dirt, just outside their town, and found a dinosaur egg. According to the report, the children sold the egg to a museum for thousands of dollars.

But the story possibilities are many. Discuss with your students:

- What if it was you who found a dinosaur egg?
- What would you do with it?
- What if you could hatch that dinosaur egg, because in stories anything is possible.
- Could you write a poem about a dinosaur? Or a poem about a child hatching a dinosaur egg?

Teens Stranded on Island for Three Weeks

This report tells of three teenagers who took their canoe out on a huge lake. They stopped at a little island and, while they were there, their canoe drifted away. The children were presumed drowned but in reality lived stranded on the tiny island for three weeks before they were found.

Here are some questions to ask your students to answer:

- What if that had happened to you and your best friends?
- What would you do? What would you eat? How would you feel?
- How would your friendships change?
- Could you write poem about loneliness?
- About the things you'd miss?
- Can you write a poem about being stranded on an island?

Dogs feature in many wild articles, as demonstrated by some of the other articles I have:

- A dog who is trained to dial 9-1-1 when his owner needs medical help.
- A dog who swallowed a cell phone and was heard "ringing" when the number was dialed!
- "Goose Thinks He's a Dog," about a goose who frequents a schoolyard to play with the children and who barks like a dog, too.
- "Dog Gone," the story of a chihuahua in Alaska who was carried off by a bald eagle.
- And I have an article about a stray dog who found a lost little boy in the woods, kept him warm, and barked until the rescuers found him!

You get the idea: so many wonderful true stories, just waiting to be turned into poetry by your students!

A Few More Thoughts to Share. . .

- If your classroom situation allows it, whenever your students are engaged in a writing activity, *please* write along with the kids. There is no stronger message than modeling what you want them to do. If you tell your students how important poetry is and then sit down to do some marking, your good intentions will fall flat. Please write and indulge in the joy of poetry yourself. Don't be embarrassed to share your writing, your thoughts, your sentiments with the students. There is no lesson more powerful than having them see that you like to write, that you like their writing and that, sometimes, you cry about a memory! Your participation will forge strong bonds between you and your fellow poets.

- When you and your students are sharing poems, please don't make each student get up and read aloud. This can cause some kids to "hate" poetry! Only let those students read aloud who want to. Offer that you or someone else can read a reluctant student's writing or don't share it aloud at all. Students reluctant to read their poems aloud might warm up to the sharing idea later as they gain confidence in their writing ability.

- As your students complete poems, store them in a binder or file folder for future editing and/or publishing.

- Before your students start writing, stress that they should focus on writing what they *want to say* and not to stop to worry about neatness, spelling, grammar, or punctuation. At this stage of development, the focus during the creative writing process should be on conveying the intended message or sounds. Students should realize that *they* are in charge of crafting the poem. They can edit their writing after they complete the first draft. Editing will improve their writing but it is more important, for now, to be creative and to let their imaginations soar.

Chapter 2 Bibliography and Web Sties

Bibliography

Alligator Pie, by Dennis Lee. Toronto: Macmillan of Canada, 1974.

Aster Aardvark's Alphabet Adventures, by Steven Kellogg. New York: Morton, 1987.

Barn Dance, by Bill Martin Jr. and John Archambault. New York: Henry Holt, 1986.

Best Witches, Poems for Halloween, by Jane Yolen. New York: G. P. Putnam's Sons, 1989.

Dinosaurs, selected by Lee Bennett Hopkins. Orlando, Fla.: HBJ, 1987.

Extra Innings, Baseball Poems, by Lee Bennett Hopkins. San Diego, Calif.: Harcourt Brace, 1993.

Hoops, by Robert Burleigh. San Diego, Calif.: Harcourt, Brace, 1997.

Hurray for Dieffendoofer Day! by Dr. Seuss and Jack Prelutsky. New York: Alfred A. Knopf, 1998.

I Can Read with My Eyes Shut, by Dr. Seuss. New York, Random House.

If I Had a Paka, by Charlotte Pomerantz. New York, Greenwillow Books.

I Know an Old Laddie, by Jean Little. Toronto: Viking.

Jelly Belly, by Dennis Lee. Macmillan of Canada, 1983.

Literature & the Learner, by Frances S. Goforth. Wadsworth, 1998.

Oh, the Places He Went, by Maryann N. Weidt. Minneapolis, Minn.: Carolrhoda Books, 1994.

Poetry Party, by Bruce Lansky. Meadowbrook Press, 1996.

Rainbows, Head Lice and Pea Green Tile: Poems in the Voice of the Classroom Teacher, by Brod Bagert. Gainesville, Fla.: Maupin House, 1999.

Red Dog Blue Fly, Football Poems, by Sharon Bell Mathis. New York: Viking.

Scared Silly! A Book for the Brave, by Marc Brown. Boston: Little, Brown, 1994.

Something Big Has Been Here, by Jack Prelutsky. New York: Scholastic, 1992.

The Alphabet from Z to A: (With Much Confusion on the Way), by Judith Viorst. Atheneum, 1994.

The Bat Poet, By Randall Jarrell, illustrated by Maurice Sendak. HarperCollins, 1996.

The Best of Robert Service, by Robert Service. Toronto: McGraw Hill Ryerson.

The Cremation of Sam McGee, by Robert Service, illustrated by Ted Harrison. Toronto: Kids Can Press, 1986.

The D- Poems of Jeremy Bloom, by Gordon Korman and Bernice Korman. New York: Scholastic, 1992.

The Eleventh Hour, by Graeme Base. Stoddart, Canada, 1988.

The Ice Cream Store, by Dennis Lee. HarperCollins, 1991.

The Last Place Sports Poems of Jeremy Bloom, by Gordon Korman and Bernice Korman. New York: Scholastic, 1996.

The Sign of the Sea Horse, by Graeme Base. Doublebase Pty., 1992.

The Worst Band in the Universe, by Graeme Base. Doubleday Canada, 1999.

There Was an Old Woman, by Steven Kellogg. New York: Four Winds Press.

Toes in My Nose and Other Poems, by Sheree Fitch. Toronto: Doubleday Canada, 1987.

Virtual Maniac, by Margriet Ruurs. Gainesville, Fla.: Maupin House, 2000.

What's on the Menu? selected by Bobbye S. Goldstein. New York: Viking, 1992.

Web Sites

http://www.usatoday.com/news/nweird.htm (*USA Today,* "Weird News")

For more uses of newspapers in the classroom, check out Newspapers in Education (N.I.E.) in your area or: http://www.pilotonlilne. com/nie

CHAPTER 3

Writing Activities

Prewriting Activity 1 — Wordstorming!

> The aims of this activity are to generate a wide selection of words and to expand vocabulary.

Start by choosing a topic—any topic. Say, "We are going to find words to describe. . ."

You can choose any topic at all; here are a few to help you get started.

- weather
- holidays
- cars
- music
- people
- food

These are pretty broad topics. Get more specific if you want:

- sunshine
- beach
- speed
- a piano
- my best friend
- chocolate

Decide on your topic and write it on the board. Let's say we chose "chocolate." (my favorite!) Now ask your students to wordstorm. Which words come to mind when they try to describe chocolate? Write down all responses: brown, yummy, hard, sweet, melting, sharing, mouth-watering. When they seem to run out of descriptive words, start asking questions that will generate more words. Write them all down!

- What does it taste like? (good, velvety, smooth)
- What does it look like when it melts? (brown mud, flowing liquid, like my skin, decadent)
- What does it taste like when you take a bite? (forbidden fruit, heavenly, so sweet, scrumptious, luscious)

Keep asking questions and prodding for more words until the well runs dry! Once your board is covered in words, and students' vocabularies start to be depleted, invite them to write poems using some of the words on the board. If your students have never written poetry, you may want to offer the choice of writing a poem or a short story. But you'll be amazed to see how they use these wordstorms.

Wordstorm often. The activity will increase your students' vocabularies and open their eyes to the possibilities of a poem. When students have written a poem or a short story, ask them to share their writing out loud so others can hear what they did with the words, the same words they all heard. The variety of how they use these same words will be amazing. Once your students get used to the concept of wordstorming, they can start to suggest their own topics to wordstorm.

Prewriting Activity 2 — Generating Ideas

> The aim of this acitivity is to help students realize they have stories to tell—from their everyday lives, from books they have read, and more.

An idea is the first thing you need when you want to write. What will you write about? The "idea" is perhaps the most important part of the poem. Without ideas, there wouldn't be poems or story lines. So, it's important to explore the "getting ideas" stage of the writing process.

When a student is assigned the task of writing a poem, or a story for that matter, where does he or she find an idea for what to write about? When I visit a school, the most frequently asked question is, "Where do you get your ideas?" Where *do* ideas come from? And how can you help students generate ideas?

Start off by talking about the importance of keeping track of ideas. Suggest to your students that they use a specific scribbler, a binder, or any kind of notebook dedicated to keeping track of ideas. Encourage them to jot down ideas whenever and wherever they get them: on the school bus, in class, at home, just before falling asleep. I keep a pen with a built-in little light next to my bed, just to record those great ideas that sneak in at night!

Ask your students to start a new page or sheet of paper and write the heading *Ideas* on it. Invite them to jot down any ideas they get, while you talk. Show them how to jot down two or three words to help them remember a particular idea. A notation can be as short as "finding dinosaur egg" or "going to the pool"—just enough to help the student remember that good idea when the time comes to write the poem itself. Discussions with your students about where to get ideas might include the following:

- You can get an idea from reading other books. Reading one poem can trigger ideas for a different poem about a similar topic, but never copy a poem.

- You can get an idea while watching a movie or a sitcom on TV. Write your idea down or it will be gone by the time the show is over!

- Dreams can be a good source of ideas. Try to recall the story you dreamt or use fragments of dreams in your writing.

- Something that actually happened to you is an excellent source of ideas. It is a good idea to write about something you know. If you really went skiing, maybe you can write a ski poem, a snow poem, a cold poem. If you went on an airplane, can you write a poem about traveling, flying, clouds, a suitcase, a foreign country?

I traveled on an airplane once and wrote a poem about clouds. Later it was published in an airline magazine for kids. Another time I was waiting in the airport of Medicine Hat, Alberta, when a cat rubbed up against my suitcase. When I asked what a cat was doing in the airport, I was told that he lived there; they even called him "our airport cat." So, I wrote a poem called *The Airport Cat of Medicine Hat* and it was published, too. Maybe you really have a dog. Why not write a poem about him? (And, of course remind your students to write down their ideas while you talk!)

- Maybe you get an idea from something someone says. Someone may say one funny word that you might want to write a poem about. Or they might say something that will give you a complete story idea. Little kids especially are great at saying funny things that can be turned into poems. If your students have younger brothers or sisters, or if they baby-sit, your students can listen to the funny things the younger kids say. I have a whole notebook full of funny things my own kids said when they were little. Things like:

  - "I was born in a hopsetall."

  - Pointing to the stamp of the Queen of England on a parcel that came in the mail, he said, "It's from Grandma! Grandma put her picture on it!"

  - "Why is a dragonfly called a dragonfly? Can it breathe fire?"

  - "Where does the white go when the snow melts?"

Prewriting Activity 3 — Generating Ideas — "What If. . ."

> The aims of this activity are to generate ideas and to help the students realize their sense of imagination.

Two simple words can spark a myriad of ideas. Say, "What if. . . ," and the range of poem possibilities becomes endless.

Use the following books as examples when discussing this subject:

  - What if. . . wolves could talk? (*Little Red Riding Hood*)

- What if. . . you were in a plane crash and had to survive on your own in the wilderness? (*Hatchet,* by Gary Paulsen)
- What if. . . you met a ghost? (*Awake and Dreaming,* by Kit Pearson)
- What if. . . a mitten could keep animals warm in winter? (*The Mitten,* by Jan Brett)
- What if. . . you turned out to be a princess (*A Royal Pain,* by Ellen Conford)

Discuss with your students how real events may lead to poetry when imagination is added.

- What if. . . you got to go to Disneyland?
- What if. . . you met a movie star?
- Perhaps you really have a horse. What if. . . you won a race?
- Maybe you really have a dog, what if. . . he rescued a child?
- Maybe you really went downhill skiing. What if. . . you witness a mysterious person near a cabin in the backcountry?
- Ask your students to make their own "What If" list. These ideas will be in addition to the "Ideas" list they made before. What If ideas tend to be more fantasy.

Keep the lists handy for when your students start to write.

Now that they have a supply of wonderful ideas from which to choose, let's start to write poems.

Writing Activity 1 — Inside Me

> The aim of this activity is to help students use personal thoughts and feelings as writing resources.

A great way to start off the school year (or to get to know students in the classroom in which you are the substitute teacher) is to ask students to write about who they are as an "Inside Me" poem. Explain to them that there is more inside them than organs and blood. What makes them tick? What gets them excited? What do they do outside school? Are they passionate about sports, music?

Who are their family members? What are their dreams, their aspirations?

You might want to introduce yourself to the students by writing your own "Inside Me" poem prior to this session. Write your "Inside Me" poem from the heart, while focusing on what you like and dislike. Forget about trying to be the best poet in the world. Forget about all the writing rules you know! Write from the heart, then share your poem with the kids.

Now invite the students to tell you about *themselves* in a poem called "Inside Me" or "What I'm All About." Explain to them that their poems can rhyme or not rhyme. Poems need not rhyme to be poems! (By the way, did you know that there is such a thing as a rhyming dictionary?! You can use one to find rhyming *ends* to words. Instead of looking up the first letters of a word, you look for similar-sounding endings. Look for a rhyming dictionary in the library or bookstore and see if you, or your students, find it helpful in writing poetry.)

Here are two examples of "Inside Me" poems.

Inside Me

Inside me, I'm with old friends
singing and laughing, having fun.
Inside me, I'm playing outside
swinging on a swing, playing soccer.
Inside me, the sun shines everyday.
Later I'm alone again but that's okay
Any day with my friends is a perfect day.

(Natalie, age 9)

Inside Me

Inside me there is fun
I like to play sports and I like to run.
There is snow inside of me.
I don't think about the past.
I like to live every day
as if it were my last.

(Jeremy, Grade 6)

You will notice that, even though I did give the students a topic and even a suggested title, they were free to decide *what* about them is important and what aspect of themselves they want to talk about. Sharing these poems in the classroom might show a completely different side to their fellow students.

But, please, don't ever force a student to share his or her writing. Writing, especially writing poetry, can be a very private activity. Students should always be able to elect *not* to read out loud.

Writing Activity 2 — "What If. . ."

> The aims of this activity are to stimulate the students' imaginations and to increase their awareness of storytelling.

Some "What If" poems to share with your students include

"What If. . .," by Isabel Joshlin Glaser. From: *Dinosaurs*, selected by Lee Bennett Hopkins.
"If I Were The Teacher," by Margriet Ruurs. From: *Virtual Maniac*.
"If You Should Meet," by Dennis Lee. From: *Alligator Pie*.

Ask your students to take out their "What If" lists. Those two magical words can be very helpful if you want to write poetry. Ask your students to pick one of their ideas to now write a poem about. Or they can write a poem with an opening sentence that starts with "What if. . ." Encourage them to let their imaginations run wild while writing this poem!

The "What If's" might include:

- What if you won a million dollars. . .
- What if you could go to the moon. . .
- What if lollipops grew on trees. . .
- What if you tripped a bank robber. . .

Allow approximately thirty minutes for students to decide on their topic and write the first draft of their poem. Invite students to read aloud their poems for other students to hear. This will generate more ideas for the next writing period.

Writing Activity 3 — Tongue Twisters and Non-Sense

The aim of this activity is to demonstrate specific use of language.

This is a fun activity to start off your school year with poetry and excite students about playing with language. Reading tongue twisters can lead to writing your own! From your book display choose samples of funny, silly tongue twisters, such as:

- "Jilliky Jolliky Jelliky Jee," by Jack Prelutsky. From: *Ride A Purple Pelican.*

- "The Blug in the Plug," by Sheree Fitch. From: *Toes in My Nose.*

- "A Magic Chant," by Bobbi Katz. From: *Scared Silly!*, selected by Marc Brown.

- "Peter Ping and Patrick Pong," by Dennis Lee. From: *The Ice Cream Store.*

Once they have heard lots of fun language, invite the students to choose their favorite letter of the alphabet, or to use the first letter of their name.

Have them write a list of words that begin with that letter. The list should include nouns and verbs.

Now invite students to compose a tongue twister using most of the words. The tongue twisters can rhyme or not rhyme.

Blue Drew

Drew blew a blue picture
and blew blue bubble gum
He wore a bright blue sweater
that reached down to his bum!

(Natalie, Grade 4)

Silly Sally

Silly singing Sally
sat on a swing
singing a super silly song!

(Chelsey, Grade 5)

Reading the tongue twisters out loud gives the children a wonderful taste of poetry. They discover that playing with words is fun, and that they can do it! Making silly tongue twisters that make others laugh gives them a sense of power. Word power!

They'll enjoy the sounds and the wordplay. They start to realize that any form of rhythmic language is poetry and marvel at it. They'll find joy in discovering words and rhythms.

After having written and shared short tongue twisters, you might want to read a longer, epic poem that celebrates nonsense words, such as:

- *Jabberwocky*, by Lewis Carroll.
- *Yertle the Turtle*, by Dr. Seuss.
- *The Whingdingdilly*, by Bill Peet.
- "The Quangle Wangle's Hat," by Edward Lear. From: *The Complete Nonsense of Edward Lear.*

Assign your students to write more tongue twisters as they become inspired by the language in these poems. After I read *The Jabberwocky* to a group of students, Jackie wrote this poem:

My Trull is So Drab

My trull is so drab
the drabbest drull
you ever saw
My bull is sob
the sabbest bull
you ever saw.

(Jackie, Grade 7)

Writing Activity 4 — Awesome Alliteration

> The aim of this activity is to increase poetry writing skills through alliteration.

Here are some poems that use alliteration:

- "The Pig in Pink Pajamas," by Dennis Lee. From: *The Ice Cream Store.*
- "Moose Meadow," by Margriet Ruurs. From: *Virtual Maniac.*
- "A Vote For Vanilla," by Eve Merriam. From: *What's on the Menu?,* selected by Bobbye S. Goldstein.
- "The Meal," by Karla Kuskin. From: *What's on the Menu?,* selected by Bobbye S. Goldstein.
- *Aster Aardvark's Alphabet Adventures*, by Steven Kellogg.
- "Snowflake Soufflé," by X. J. Kennedy. From: *For Laughing Out Loud*, selected by Jack Prelutsky.

In the previous activity, students experienced the fun of working with sounds. Let's broaden their options and introduce them to the technique of *alliteration*. Explain to your students that using words beginning with the same sounds is alliteration. Write a list of examples on the board and solicit more suggestions from the students. Be sure to include alliteration made by both beginning vowels as well as consonants:

- big brown bear
- mountain magic
- the terrible twos
- eight elegant elephants
- the sun set slowly
- shine and shade
- flying flamingos

You can make a list of name alliterations for characters to use in later poems. Some suggestions:

- Wild Willy of the West
- Principal Peters
- Miss Muffins

–   <u>S</u>illy <u>S</u>imon
–   <u>J</u>umping <u>J</u>ack

You could even come up with an alliteration for each letter of the alphabet.

Now ask your students to write a poem using any of the listed alliterations or to invent new ones to write a **Perfect Poem**! Have fun sharing them.

Writing Activity 5 — Rhythm and Rhyme

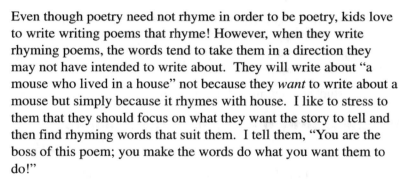

The aim of this activity is to increase poetry writing skills through awareness of rhythm and rhyme.

Even though poetry need not rhyme in order to be poetry, kids love to write writing poems that rhyme! However, when they write rhyming poems, the words tend to take them in a direction they may not have intended to write about. They will write about "a mouse who lived in a house" not because they *want* to write about a mouse but simply because it rhymes with house. I like to stress to them that they should focus on what they want the story to tell and then find rhyming words that suit them. I tell them, "You are the boss of this poem; you make the words do what you want them to do!"

Here are some techniques that help to generate rhyme.

It is easy to find words that rhyme if you remove the first letter of the word and substitute another letter of the alphabet until the letters make a suitable word:

band	hand
land	stand
sand	

Write commonly used words, such as these, on the board and ask students to find a rhyming word for each:

head	dog	boy	home	scared
tear	house	happy	car	train

Now ask the students to pick some of these words and write a rhyming poem with them.

You can also switch the words of a *sentence* around to find a better word to rhyme with. If the line that you want to rhyme with says,

" all night the dog <u>barked</u>"

and you can't find a word to rhyme with "barked," maybe you can change the sentence around and say,

"the dog barked all <u>night</u>"

and now you can rhyme with "<u>right</u>" or "<u>fight</u>."

You could also change the sentence so that it says,

"all the dog did was <u>bark</u>"

and now you can rhyme with "<u>dark</u>" or "<u>shark</u>" or "<u>park</u>"!

If you have a rhyming dictionary, **(see page 36)** your students might want to use it for this activity. There is also a web site with an on-line rhyming dictionary: http://rhyme.lycos.com/. Type in any word and it will find words that rhyme.

Ask your students to write a rhyming poem.

Writing Activity 6 — Painting Pictures with Words

> The aim of this activity is to increase writing skills through appropriate use of language.

Kids often think that "if it doesn't rhyme it isn't poetry." So, let's specifically write some non-rhyming poetry. Discovering that poetry need not rhyme can bring a kind of *freedom* to a young author. Since rhyming tends to take students in a different direction from the intended story, experimenting with non-rhyming poetry frees them to concentrate on what they really *want* the poem to say. Emphasize to your students that *they* are in charge of the words, not the other way around. They need to choose words that "paint the right picture." The target, when painting mind pictures, is to make someone else (the reader) feel what you (the writer) feel. Using the right words helps to accomplish that.

This activity helps students understand that poems need not rhyme. Start by reading a variety of non-rhyming poetry, including:

- *Hoops,* by Robert Burleigh.
- "The Wind of Spring," by Myra Cohn Livingston. From: *Make Things Fly,* selected by Dorothy M. Kennedy.
- "Quiet Storm," by Lydia Okutoro. From: *Quiet Storm.*
- "The Ocean," by Margriet Ruurs. From: *Virtual Maniac.*
- "Poor Ron's Allergy," by Brod Bagert. From: *Let Me Be the Boss.*
- *Owl Moon,* by Jane Yolen.

This activity makes children aware of how poetry differs from prose visually and of the specific choices of words and patterns in poetry. Have them rewrite any poem in their own words as a story. Then consider how the two ways of telling the story differ. This practice helps them experience what makes a poem: shorter sentences, rhythmic and condensed language, and sometimes rhyme—but not necessarily.

Let's do this as a group activity with the whole class.

STEP 1. Use the following poem:

Campfire Time

The crackling campfire dances
with long, licking flames,
while we sing silly songs
and play a million games.

Snapping, crackling twigs
compete with blazing fire
as glowing firefly sparks
dance higher and higher.

Teasing, threatening,
golden tongues lick
at the dark of night
and at my marshmallow stick.

(Margriet Ruurs, from *Virtual Maniac*)

Write the poem on your board or a flip chart. Read it out loud with they students.

STEP 2. Now ask them to tell you what is happening and record the event as a story, like a reporter who was there to observe. Prod them with questions if need be (Where? When? Who? What?). This kind of description will emerge:

> It was night time. A group of people was sitting around a campfire. They were singing and telling stories. The fire was making noise and sending off sparks. They were also roasting marshmallows.

STEP 3. Look at how the two accounts differ:

- Point out the use of shorter lines in the poem. Even if one whole verse is one sentence, it has been broken into shorter chunks.

- Find the places where the technique of alliteration was used in the poem. Did we use alliteration in the description?

- Does the poem rhyme? Determine the rhyme scheme.

- Which account paints a better picture in your head?

STEP 4. Since this poem happens to rhyme, let's re-write it as a non-rhyming poem to demonstrate that it will still be poetry:

Campfire Time

Crackling campfire dances
with long, licking flames
as we sit under the blanket of night
and try counting stars in the sky.

Snapping, crackling twigs
compete with blazing fire
as glowing sparks dance
their own campfire song.

Teasing, threatening,
golden tongues lick
at the black of night
and lap up the darkness.

STEP 5. Compare the rhyming and the non-rhyming versions of the poem. Which do you prefer? Why? How do their sounds differ? Do they paint different pictures?

STEP 6. Invite your students to write their own non-rhyming poem. They can try to rewrite a rhyming poem they wrote previously. Or they can decide to write a non-rhyming poem about any topic: nature, a memory, something funny, something sad, a place, a person, anything at all!

If they need help coming up with a topic to write about, you can supply pictures from your picture file, suggest a recent event or experience, ask your students to describe their pet or have a look at their 'Idea' or "What If" lists.

Here is one of my favorite non-rhyming poems written by a fourth grader.

First Snow

One morning as I awoke
I looked outside and saw
the first snow had come
like a great cloud of white
settled over the country.
It was early morning
no footprints in the snow
Just a velvet carpet of white.
I got up, hurried to be the first
to jump and roll and make my impression.
It was cold outside
but that did not matter
It had snowed
That's what mattered.

(Emily, age 9)

Writing Activity 7 — Nature Poetry

> The aims of this activity are to increase
> vocabulary and to write from memory.

Here are some nature poems to read with your students:

- "Owls in the Wood," by Margriet Ruurs. From: *Virtual Maniac.*

- "The Wind was on the Withered Heath," by J. R. R. Tolkien. From: *The Magic Tree.*

- "Eons, Hours and Wind," by Brod Bagert. From: *Let Me Be the Boss.*

- *Aska's Animals,* by Warabé Aska and David Day.

After sharing such poems by your favorite authors, ask your students write some nature poems. Invite your students to close their eyes and recall a special place they knew:

- a wintery trail on a snowy hill;

- a spot in the sun by a sparkling river,

- a sturdy branch of a tree they like to sit in

and to write about that spot. I ask them to really concentrate on that place, using all of their senses: sound, smell, touch, hearing, as well as sight. You may need to spend ten minutes or so talking about the scenes, the possibilities. Try to create a relaxed, quiet atmosphere.

Now invite the students to write a poem about the place they pictured in their head. Urge them not to worry about correct spelling or grammar rules. It is important to focus on the essence of the story line.

If they have trouble thinking of such a place or event, supply them with pictures of nature paintings. I use pictures which show animals and flowers in mountain settings, photos of farm animals, a flower in bloom, dew drops on the grass, and so on.

Taking your class out into nature, such as a field trip or even just under a tree on the school grounds, may motivate good nature poems.

If your classroom situation allows, participate in the activity by writing your own poem. Let the children write for as long as most remain quiet. When most are done, invite the students to share. You might want to start off by reading the poem you wrote or by offering to read a particularly well written poem by a shy student who volunteers. It won't be long before they'll be eager to share their writing.

Follow-up activities might include painting an illustration to accompany the poem. Pictures and poems can be displayed on a wall.

Blue Flower

Blue flower growing in a corn field,
you look so out of place
Growing in a field of gold
you hold up your head with grace.

(Tara, Grade 6)

Writing Activity 8 — Music is Poetry

> The aim of this activity is to create awareness of language use in lyrics.

All songs are poems. If you take away the tune, you are left with the lyrics. Lyrics make wonderful, often rhyming, poetry. Listen to songs in your classroom by bringing in a tape deck. You might want to select well known songs suited for your students, including:

- "Baby Beluga" (Raffi)
- "Heal The World" (Michael Jackson)
- "If" (Roger Whittaker)
- "Yesterday" (The Beatles)

I like the lyrics of some songs by Savage Garden, Elton John, the Spice Girls and Boy Zone. The text of the songs from *The Lion King* are very cleverly crafted. With older students, try listening to texts by Leonard Cohen. My particular favorite song text is "The Music of the Night" from *The Phantom of the Opera*. It's a great poem.

STEP 1. Select a song with good lyrics. Listen to the entire song once with your students, then play the song again and stop the tape at short intervals so that your students can listen to the text. Ask a few students to record the words on paper.

STEP 2. Read the song as a poem. How is it different when spoken? Which parts of the text had they picked up on already? Which rhyming words did they notice?

You may want to ask students to bring in a favorite piece of music. They will enjoy listening to their own music and choosing their favorite lyrics to share with the class.

STEP 3. Now ask your students to pick a poem they have written, or invite them to write a poem specifically for this activity. When the poem is completed, try to put it to a tune. They can select their own favorite genre. One student may want to hum his or her song to a country tune. Others might want to get together and rap their poem.

Students could be teamed up to produce songs and perform them.

As an example of how poems can be put to music, show your students the book *Ride a Purple Pelican,* by Jack Prelutsky. Get the taped version of this book from your library to hear how each poem is presented as a song. A wide variety of tunes is used to sing each poem.

Writing Activity 9 — And Poetry is Music!

> The aims of this activity are to write creatively and to increase poetry skills.

Instrumental music works well in inspiring children to write. Setting the mood for this writing activity is very important. Invite the students to get into a comfortable position in their chairs or even on the floor. Create a cozy, relaxed atmosphere in the classroom by closing blinds or dimming fluorescent lights.

Make sure students are equipped with paper and pencils that won't need sharpening for a while. Play quiet, instrumental music. Selections can include instrumental versions of Broadway shows, classical music by Tschaikovsky, Strauss, Mozart, and examples of other musical genres. Ask students to listen to the music, to let the music start to paint a picture in their mind. Then they can start writing a poem about the scene they see in their heads while listening to the music. Make the activity last for as long as the students' attention span will keep them listening and writing.

Here's a poem one seventh grader wrote while listening to instrumental music:

Flamingos

An unfolded treasure blooming in sparkling water,
silky flowers bursting from a deep sleep,
Magical rose crayons scribble on swift paper,
light flamingos dance under the tender moon.

(Tara, Grade 7)

Writing Activity 10 — Poems That Tell Stories

The aim of this activity is to learn narrative writing skills.

Books/poems to read include:
- *There's a Mouse in My House*, by Sheree Fitch
- *The Sign of the Sea Horse*, by Graeme Base
- *The Cremation of Sam McGee,* by Robert Service
- *Two by Two*, by Barbara Reid
- *The Party*, by Barbara Reid

Read one of the suggested narrative poems and discuss the elements that make it different from a descriptive poem, which does not tell a story, but paints a picture or evokes a feeling. Discuss the beat of the poem. Listen for the beat. Read the verses in an exaggerated manner and have the kids clap their hands to the beat.

After you have shared epic poems like *The Cremation of Sam McGee* and *The Eleventh Hour* with your students, ask them to write their own "story poem"—a tale told in rhyme format. Share the poems through classroom readings.

Topics/titles can include:

- The Ballad of.................. (your school name)
- The Voyage of the Seventh Grade (about a field trip)
- legend topics such as "How the Tiger Got His Tail" or "How the Zebra Got His Stripes."

Here is an example of a poem written by one of my students that tells a story:

Shipwrecked

I went to an island
a long ways away.
It remains undiscovered
to this very day.

I landed on this island.
You see, I was shipwrecked
on a long sailing voyage
as far as I recollect.

The ship's name I cannot remember
nor any of the crew.
I saw no animals
so ate leaves and bamboo.

Then I found some natives
who praised me and called me Zeus.
I sat there thinking
that I could put this to use.

I lived there for some 20 years
My story told to few.
And I give you this privilege:
I tell it now to you.

(Marcus, Grade 7)

Writing Activity 11 — Metaphor and Simile

> The aim of this activity is to learn the poetry
> writing techniques of metaphor and simile.

Poetry is like porridge: it warms the body and the soul. Metaphors
and similes can be a strong part of poetry. Kids love using metaphor and simile, often doing so even if they are not familiar with
the terms. The concept of metaphor is something they frequently
already use unconsciously. Even very young writers, unfamiliar
with the definitions, will understand the idea.

Explain to your students that when we compare two things and say
they are "like" each other it is called a *simile*. ("The rain fell like
tears.") In a *metaphor*, dissimilar things are compared without the
word "like." ("The moon was a beckoning lantern.")

Metaphor

The dragon in the poem is the ocean, but it's never directly stated:

The Ocean

A giant dragon,
breathing foam
on rocky, green toes.

It roars,
then softly rumbles,
retreats to attack again.

It gathers misty breath
and strength
to roar back with all its might
and eat away at sand and caves,
its belly softly rumbling.

It rests.
Gray back panting, heaving,
rise and fall, it slumbers
then wakes again and roars,
spitting foam and salty mist.

(Margriet Ruurs, *Virtual Maniac*)

When you write a metaphor, you use your imagination to describe it. I compared the ocean to a dragon. You could call a storm "a fierce lion" or a flower "a yellow symphony." Brainstorm with your students what other comparisons you could make. Make a list of similes and metaphors on the blackboard. For example:

- My kitten is like a powder puff
- Homework is like eating spinach
- Sunshine is like honey
- Icy teeth hung off the roof

Make a list of *real* things and then write a metaphor for that word:

It *really* is:	It *could* be called:
storm	lion

Now invite your students to pick one metaphor and write a metaphor poem!

Here's one of my favorites. Sarah compared "the wind" to "angels" in her poem:

The Wind

The angels sing their haunting tunes,
wailing high and low.
They sweep between the maple trees,
as on and on they blow.
The angels' gray and foggy skirts
are dragging through the grass.
And as I look out my window,
By and by they pass.

(Sarah, Grade 7)

Simile

Flying Free

I know that if I really try,
deep down I *know* that I can fly!
Standing on a fence,
flapping with my hands,
I'll soar through the sky,
like a bird I will fly.

Floating free as a cloud
over treetops I'll sail about,
I know that if I really try,
deep down I know
that I can fly!
So, here I go!

(Margriet Ruurs)

"Like a bird I will fly," the poem says.

What other expressions do we use to compare ourselves to animals?

Can your students think of some? Write all suggestions down on the blackboard.

Did they think of "quiet as a mouse"? "Gentle as a lamb"? We say, "You swim like a fish" and "He is strong as bear." Save the list of animal similes you now have for use in future poems.

Invite your students to write down other common similes. Now ask them to choose one simile and write a poem about it. They might choose to write a poem about being strong as a horse, roaring like a lion, or swimming like a fish!

"Guess What?"

It is fun to turn metaphor poetry into a game by writing poems and asking each other to guess what it *really* is about. Ask your students to think of a subject and then decide what it is *like*. This is similar to how I decided that the ocean is like a dragon. If your students need warming up to this activity, discuss more examples, list them on the board, and allow your students to use those. Here are some suggestions:

- Spring could be "a butterfly."
- Rain could be "tears."
- Worries can be "a heavy package" or "a suitcase."

One of my students wrote about a rainbow, calling it a smile in the sky:

Rainbow

Something is way up high
an upside-down smile in the sky.
After the tears go
the upside-down smile starts to glow.

(Chelsey, Grade 4)

To demonstrate the guessing element, read this poem to your students without revealing the title. Ask them to guess what it is about.

Now ask your students to write their poems but when sharing, not to reveal the true subject. Turn the sharing of the poems into a guessing game by inviting the rest of the class to guess the real topic of each poem!

Writing Activity 12 — Fortunately Poetry!

The aim of this activity is to offer poetry writing experience.

Turn poetry writing into a tasty subject. Buy a bag of fortune cookies, enough to have one cookie for each student in your group. This next part is a little bit tedious but well worth the effort! With a pair of tweezers, remove the original slip of paper from each fortune cookie and discard. Write a short sentence, or just a noun with an adjective, on little slips of paper. The words you choose

can be random or you may decide on a theme. Fold and insert one
into each fortune cookie.

Have your students break open their cookie and write a poem about
the words, *or* starting with the words, they find. Delicious poetry
will follow!

Use your own imagination to write sentences or use these samples:

- The galloping horse. . .
- Softly falling snow
- The giggling girl
- Gentle lapping water
- The strong man lifted the child
- Which puppy to choose
- A happy smile greeted me
- Six silly sisters
- It shook and it creaked
- The road was windy up ahead
- The cat curled up and. . .
- The wind howled as. . .
- Slowly I opened the book

Writing Activity 13 — Poetry Workout

> The aim of this activity is to increase
> students' confidence in their writing skills.

Here is a fun writing activity that will get even the most reluctant
student excited about writing. Students can write either poems or
short stories.

What you need

- an old, discarded dictionary (pick them up from used book
  sales, garage sales, etc.)

- a sheet of lined paper and a pencil per student

- something to ring at the start and finish (I use a Swiss cow
  bell; you could use any kind of bell, an alarm clock, an egg
  timer, a horn, a whistle, even a bicycle bell!)

STEP 1. Explain to the students that you are now going to do a "poetry workout." Workouts are meant to exercise your body, but this one will give your brain a workout! Briefly explain the process as it is outlined below. Emphasize to your students that they may not complete a finished piece of writing. Explain that this exercise is merely an activity to have fun with words and to help them discover how well they can write in a very short time! They will be amazed at what they can do!

STEP 2. Explain steps 2-4 to your students before you do them. When the process is clear, proceed.

Go around the classroom and let students tear out a page of your old dictionary. Let them pick a page, any page, and rip it out! They immediately have to put their page under their sheet of writing paper, without peeking at it! It is important to explain this well beforehand. They should all start at the same time, so they should not look at their page yet!

STEP 3. Once all students have received a page from the old dictionary, you will ring your bell. When the bell rings, students are to take out their ripped page, scan the page for words, and choose *any* word from their page.

NOTE: It is important that they realize they can use *any* word, not just the bold ones listed in alphabetical order. They can use any word or combination of words or short phrase of their choice, as long as it appears somewhere on the page, on either side.

STEP 4. At this point you may have to walk from desk to desk pointing out good words. Once the student has decided on his or her word, that word becomes his or her topic. The student should quickly think about the story he or she wants to tell about this topic—beginning, middle, end (even if it is a poem). The student then starts writing, without pausing to worry about spelling or punctuation.

STEP 5. Allow a reasonable amount of time based on how long students remain quiet and focused. This may be as short as ten minutes for grades 3-5; twelve to fifteen minutes for grades 6-8. You can increase the amount of time as you repeat this session and students get used to this form of writing. Ring the bell as the signal for all students to stop writing immediately.

STEP 6. Invite students to share with the rest of the group the words they chose and the poems they wrote.

Please note :

- – If students are reluctant to share, please don't force them to do so!

- – While your students are writing, and if your classroom situation allows it, pick your own page, find a word, and write your own story or poem along with them! Share it if you like—your students will be encouraged by your example, especially if your poem isn't quite perfect!

• Invite the principal or parents or anyone else in occasionally to join the students in this activity and see how much you can accomplish in a short time when you put your mind to it!

Writing Activity 14 — Personal Favorites Poetry

> The aim of this activity is to help students realize personal feelings and experiences as poetry resources.

Draw on the students' personal interests and preferences to encourage the writing of poems. Ask your students:

• What is your favorite animal?

Ask them to write a poem and share without telling the others which animal they wrote about. Can they guess it?

• What is your favorite color?

Ask them to write a poem about something of that color.

Remember that you can make up anything, even if it is not normally that color. For instance, you can write about a green cat. Or about purple and pink ice cream! Maybe you want to write about your silver race car or about your brother's yellow toes! You can even write a blue poem!

- What is your favorite food?

  Ask your students to pick their favorite food and write a poem about it! It could be about bubblegum ice cream or sloppy soup. . . or crumbly cookies or about licking licorice!

  Have delicious fun! Why not serve cookies and milk while sharing the poems!

Get in the mood by reading food poems before beginning this activity:

- "Twickham Tweer," by Jack Prelutsky. From *The Sheriff of Rottenshot.*

- "A Matter of Taste," by Eve Merriam. From: *What's on the Menu.*

- *Sleeping Dragons All Around,* by Sheree Fitch.

Writing Activity 15 — Times of Your Life

> The aim of this activity is to increase vocabulary dealing with feelings and emotions.

Ask your students to:

- think of a time in their lives, and write poems about, when they were:
  - very happy
  - scared
  - sad
  - excited

- think of a special person and write a poem about him or her.

- How about a special place? Their own room or an old house? The kitchen where your grandmother baked muffins? A tree house? Maybe it's the library or the public pool.

Ask your students:

- to write an "I remember" poem.

  - What are some of their favorite childhood memories?

  - Is it visiting a grandma? Or swinging in the playground? Or going on a trip?

- The trip to Disneyland? The sandcastle they once built? A new puppy?

Invite them to write a poem about their own, real childhood memories.

"Way Back When. . ." Poetry

Tell your students, think back to when you were little. . . You can do it if you try hard. Concentrate. . . What sort of things do you remember? What is your earliest memory? What did your bedroom look like? What kind of toys did you have? Do you remember sitting in a car seat? In a stroller? Do you remember the first time you saw the ocean or went to the fair? What was it like?

Ask them to decide on their best memories and write a poem about it.

Writing Activity 16 — Pick a Word—Any Word!

> The aim of this activity is to practice poetry writing skills.

This writing exercise uses words as a starting point.

Similar to the Poetry Workout, this workshop will give students good writing practice while having fun.

You will need:

- pieces of paper with nouns on them (a few more than you have students)
- pieces of paper with adjectives on them
- two envelopes or decorated sandwich bags
- lined paper and a pencil for each student

Type or print words clearly on the pieces of paper. Choose any kind of nouns, for example:

dinosaur	pool	boy
race car	school	backpack
books	puppy dog	hippopotamus
pirate	computer	cake

Now write your adjectives. Some examples:

purple	fast	curious
ugly	large	wiggly
sad	giggling	barking
polka dotted	funny	wide-eyed

- Put the pieces of paper with nouns in one envelope and the pieces of paper with adjectives in another envelope. Label both envelopes. Review with your students the meaning of "noun" and "adjective." Give students a sheet of paper and a pencil.

- Now let each student pick a piece of paper, one from each envelope.

  The topic of each story or poem comes from combining the pieces of paper. They will end up with funny combinations, such as a "purple dinosaur" or a "curious camel" to tell a story or poem about!

- You could also make the rule that the two words don't form the title but need to occur somewhere in the poem.

- Allow a relatively short period of time for students to write fast and furiously.

- When the students complete the writing process, encourage them to read their writing out loud.

- You can display the completed, edited writing on a wall, together with the words that were picked.

Writing Activity 17 — Picture Perfect Poems

> The aim of this activity is to use language appropriate to the format of poetry writing.

This activity uses pictures as a starting point. As suggested in the section in Chapter 2, "Making a Picture File," you may have already been collecting funny and interesting pictures.

- When you have enough pictures, explain the writing exercise to the students. Talk about the importance of illustrations in books and how pictures tell their own story. Ask them to take a close look at the picture they will get from your collection and to write the story that they think goes with it. Tell them to look for what is happening, what might have just happened, what might happen next. What is the story in this picture?

- Hand out sheets of paper and a pencil for each student.
- Go around with your envelope of pictures and let each student pick one without looking. They should quickly put their pictures under their sheets of paper without peeking.
- Once each student has a picture, you can ring your bell (to add to the sense of excitement) as a signal for the kids to take their pictures out.
- The kids should look at their pictures, quickly think of a story to tell—beginning, middle and end—and start writing. After the initial excitement there shouldn't be a lot of talking.
- When the bell rings again, students stop writing immediately. Invite them to share the pictures they picked and the poems they created.
- Display edited poems with the pictures that prompted each story.

Here is an example based on a picture that showed a museum guard dozing off on the job. A student in one of my writing workshops wrote this poem in about twelve minutes!

Museum Guard

I work in the museum,
guarding pictures where everyone can see 'em.
It's a picture made completely of tiles
I think it was made by some guy named Giles,
a picture of Romans in robes and sandals
and I have to protect it from thieves and vandals.
I was standing there, doing what I always do,
When I noticed I had to tie up my shoe.

Now while I was down there, I did not realize
that the picture started rippling, then one of those guys
stepped right out, stepped onto the floor
I'm sure that's never happened before.
In no time he was some distance away
and no one knows where he is, to this very day.
All I know is I don't have that job anymore.
I still work at the museum but now I clean the floor!

(TaraLynn, Grade 7)

Writing Activity 18 — Words That Paint Pictures

The aims of this activity are to increase vocabulary and poetry writing skills.

Poets don't use illustrations to make you see what they *want* you to see. Poets paint pictures with words. In poetry you can use language and compare things in a way that you wouldn't use in prose. Choosing the right words is especially important.

Content Cat

Pink pussycat nose
padded pussycat toes.
Swooshy black tail,
whiskers that trail,
powderpuff fur,
a pleased pussycat purr!

Ask your students to write a poem which really paints a picture in the reader's head. It can be about a cat, their dog, or anything they like! When they finish writing, let them read it out loud to a friend and ask if they see the picture the words paint in their minds. Editing after the first draft will help your students find even better words and make the image clearer.

• Invite your students to choose one of the poems they have written and to draw a picture to go with it. Drawing before and during the writing process helps your students rough out the story. Drawing is more than just doodling and can serve a real purpose.

Writing Activity 19 — [Day] Dream Poems

> The aim of this activity is to encourage the use of imagination.

Clouds

Melted marshmallow puff cloud,
floating in air, sailing about.
Cotton candy without a stick—
can I float up to take a lick?

Spoonful of whipping cream,
summerday's dream.
Can I jump in your lap
for a fleeting, float nap?

Clouds of soft cottonball fluff,
snow white bunnytail puff,
can I somersault up high
to float with you through the sky?

Discuss with your students:

• Did you ever lie on your back in the grass to watch the clouds float through the sky? Did you use your imagination to see things or animals in the shapes? Close your eyes to remember the shapes or look out of the classroom window to see clouds. Write a poem about them. You can write about one cloud and the shapes it makes. Or you can write about all the different clouds you see in the sky.

• That special time between just being awake and falling asleep is often the time you get lots of good ideas floating through your head. Do you remember the ideas when you wake up? Do you remember any dreams you had? Were they strange happenings? Can you use any dream fragments to write poems about?

A good poem to read is "Keep a Poem in your Pocket," by Beatrice Schenk de Regniers. From: *More Surprises*, selected by Lee Bennett Hopkins.

Writing Activity 20 — S-e-n-s-ible Poems

> The aims of this activity are to increase awareness of senses and to build sensory vocabulary as well as poetry writing skills.

Poems You Can Smell!

Discuss with your students:

- What are your favorite smells?
- Popcorn? Cookies? Roast beef?
- Do they bring good memories?
- Which smells do you hate? Do they bring bad memories to mind?

Smells can help to bring instant pictures to mind. Putting a smell in your poem will make a strong sensory image that people can identify with. If I describe to you the annual fair in my home-town by telling you we have a midway and animal displays, it will take me many more words to make you "see" the fair in your head than if I tell you that smells of hotdogs, popcorn, and cotton candy waft around the midway—and that you have to be careful not to step in warm cow pies when you go to see the pink piglets huddled in the sweet-smelling hay.

Think of good smells (muffins, a new puppy, a damp forest) and bad smells (hospital hallways, burning rubber). Write a poem in which smells are important!

Read: "Smelly Poem." From: *Virtual Maniac*.

A Sound Poem

Remind your students that poems don't have to rhyme to be poems. Any story, told in a rhythmic kind of way, in short sentences, is a poem.

- Let's write a poem with sounds in it: it could be wedding bells or a meowing kitten, a howling wolf or creaking branches.

- Try to write a poem that sounds like an animal. The words could ROAR, or the lines could quietly tiptoe like a mouse.

- Write a quiet or a LOUD poem!

Just for fun, read:

- "I Know All the Sounds That the Animals Make" and

- "Slow Sloth's Slow Song," by Jack Prelutsky. From: *Something Big Has Been Here*.

Feel That Poem!

Many poems deal with feelings. But did you put real feeling words into the poem? If students write about being scared, their poems will be much stronger if they *show* they were scared. As you know, the golden rule in writing is, show, don't tell! So, show "scared" by using sentences like "he felt a thousand invisible eyes on his back," "his hair stood on end and prickles ran down his spine." "She felt her skin tingle as she slowly turned and held her breath in anguish." Wordstorming (**see Prewriting Activity 1 on page 31**) will help students to increase their vocabulary about "scared" words and feelings.

Think of other feelings: embarrassed, excited, lonely, surprised, frustrated. Wordstorm and write about these feelings in a similar way.

A good sample of a poem showing "hope" is: "To You," by Langston Hughes. From: *Soul Looks Back in Wonder,* selected by Tom Feelings.

A deliciously scary poem to recite is: "What's That?" by Florence Parry Heide. From: *Scared Silly,* selected by Marc Brown.

Ask your students to write a "feelings" poem, using many words to describe *how* they feel!

Here is a poem that one of my e-mail students wrote using all senses as well as the wordplay of senses-scents:

The Scents of Christmas

The warm smell of chocolatey steam
rising from your cocoa.
The taste of colourful sprinkles
on gingerbread, warming your lips.
The feeling of a wool blanket
hugging your chilled body
sitting comfortably by the fire place.
The sight of presents in shiny paper,
the loudness of Christmas spirit surrounding
every window of carolers
with shining, smiling faces.

(Kim, Grade 8)

Writing Activity 21 — A Found Poem!

> The aim of this activity is to create awareness
> of different uses of format in writing.

Just as you can find things that become treasures, you can find words that, put together, make a poem. I'll show you and you can share this activity the same way with your students.

Here is a piece of writing:

"When I was little, Grandma's button box was my favorite toy. I would sit on the floor by Grandma's chair and she would bring me the button box. Gently, she'd bend down and put it by my feet on the carpet.

Slowly, I'd lift the lid and stare at the treasure—glittering, shimmering jewels they were. Shiny black eyes, golden coins and sparkling diamonds off princesses' dresses.

Then I'd tilt the box, slowly, with both hands until the buttons poured out onto the carpet. I'd shift them with my hands, let them run through my fingers in a cascade of colors. I'd make piles and bulldoze them around the carpet. I felt the buttons. They felt good."

Now I am going to pick words from this piece of writing and put them into a poem. I will underline the words I choose:

"When <u>I was little</u>, <u>Grandma</u>'s button box was my favorite toy. I would sit on the floor by Grandma's chair and she would bring me the button box. <u>Gently</u>, she'd bend down and put it by my feet on the carpet.

Slowly, I'd lift the lid and stare at the treasure—glittering, shimmering jewels they were. Shiny black <u>eyes</u>, golden coins and <u>sparkling</u> diamonds off princesses' dresses.

Then I'd tilt the box, slowly, with <u>both hands</u> until the buttons poured out onto the carpet. I'd shift them with <u>my hands</u>, let them run through my fingers in a cascade of colors. I'd make piles and bulldoze them around the carpet. I felt the buttons. They <u>felt good</u>."

Now I put these underlined words into a poem. Look:

Grandma

I was little
Gently
her eyes sparkled
Both hands
in my hands
Grandma felt good.

I found a poem!

Use any piece of writing for this activity. Find an essay, or copy a page from a novel for your students. Ask your students to find words and arrange them until they have found a poem.

Writing Activity 22 — Collecting Poems!

> The aims of this activity are to build poetry writing and storytelling skills.

Read:

- "The Pancake Collector," by Jack Prelutsky. From: *For Laughing Out Loud*.
- "Marcus P. Pringle," by Margriet Ruurs. From: *Virtual Maniac*.

Talk to your students about the things they like to collect.

- Baseball cards?
- Movie star photos?
- Stuffed animals?
- Marbles?

Make a list of the things they mention. Then ask them to each choose one to write a silly poem about.

Maybe it will be about an old lady who collected so many cats they wouldn't fit in the house anymore. Or about a boy who collected snakes under his bed. Or about a girl who collected rare stamps and found out one day she was rich.

I read a newspaper article about a retired school teacher who collected stamps. He took a whole bag to a stamp dealer, thinking they were worthless. But one turned out to be a very rare stamp worth $11,000!

Writing Activity 23 — Name Game

> The aim of this activity is to practice poetry techniques, such as alliteration.

Place Names

What's the name of your city? Ask your students to write a short poem about your hometown. They can use alliteration, make a tongue twister, or write a rhyming story.

Discuss unusual place names. Take out an atlas or map of your county, state, province, or country. Make a list of names of cities, lakes, mountains, etc. that appeal to you to write poems about. Here are some that I have found looking at a map:

- Quake Lake
- Ulala
- Idabel
- Parotee Point
- Blue Mud Bay
- Chocolate Lake

These names will sound wonderful in a poem. Suggest to your students that they use these (and their own) to write a poem!

For other examples of funny place names in poems, read:

- *Ride A Purple Pelican,* by Jack Prelutsky.
- "In Kamloops,"
- "Kahshe or Chicoutimi,"
- "Tongue Twister," all by Dennis Lee. From: *Alligator Pie.*
- "Kleena Kleene," by Margriet Ruurs. From: *Virtual Maniac.*

People Name Game

Use the phone book to find unusual names for people. Here are some I found in my local phone book:

- Mr. Smart, a teacher
- Mr. Book, a writer
- Dr. Pilh
- A. Bear
- Wilma Wigglesworth

Write a poem about a character using unusual names. Alliteration often works well in making up fictional names. Ask students to make up a list of fictional names. I think that "Seymour" would be a great name for an eye doctor. How about "Myrtle Mayhem"— what kind of person would she be?

Writing Activity 24 — Shape Poetry

> The aim of this activity is to play with language.

Here are two poems to read that use shapes, both from *What's on the Menu?* selected by Bobbye S. Goldstein.

- "Greedy," by Robert Froman.
- "The Baker," by Arnold Adolf.

S is for Shape!

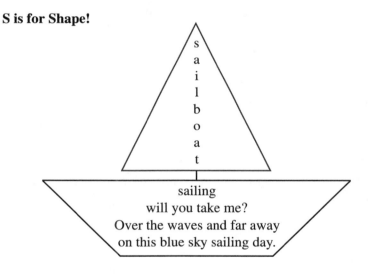

Ask your students:

- Can you write a poem that is shaped like the thing that it is about?
- Write a "normal" poem and then form the sentences into a shape.
- Use the word processor or hand write it into a shape.
- Encourage students to start off with a simple shape. They might try to write about:
  - a snake
  - an ice cream cone

- a cat
- a flower
- a house
- a piece of pie!

How about a heart-shaped Valentine Poem or a poem shaped like a Christmas tree?

As students get more experienced, try harder shapes.

Writing Activity 25 — High Interest Poems

> The aim of this activity is to make poetry writing relevant to students.

Topics that interest your students can make poetry writing relevant. What is it that your students are interested in? Is there a 'fad' game right now?

Which book is everybody reading?

Is there a good movie that they've all seen?

Find out what gets your students excited. If you have seventh grade boys, chances are they'll say, "Video games!" Try using such a topic in your writing.

Television and video can give you all sorts of ideas for stories. Invite students to think of ideas about things they've heard on TV that would make a good story or poem. Let them write a list and then see which of the ideas is suitable to write a poem about.

- You can use this topic to talk about how much television they watch and how much time they spend playing video games. Do they feel that it has an effect on them? How? Talk about positive and negative effects of watching TV and playing certain kinds of games. This discussion might give you an opportunity to discuss the level of violence in some games. How do your students feel about it? What else could make a game exciting to play?

Or you might also want to talk about the *good* news on television. What have you learned by watching TV? What happy things were on the news recently?

- Ask students to write a poem about a recent event they saw on television. This could be about a new president being elected, about someone being lost, about someone who won a lottery, etc.

- What If. . . Ask students to write about the kind of game they would create if they worked for a company that designed non-violent video games. Ask them to describe all the details, like the main characters, the places they would go, the things they would need to do, what everything looks like, etc. What would the video game be called? What would the object be?

Writing Activity 26 — Memorizing a Poem

> The aim of this activity is to practice memorization skills.

Memorizing a poem benefits students in many ways. A poem learned in childhood will stay with them for years to come. We often don't use our brains to their full capacity; learning lines from memory activates our brains.

Ask your students to choose their very favorite poems. These can be poems that they have written themselves or poems by different authors. If a poem by another author is selected, be sure credit is given when reciting it.

Recite memorized poems during class time or spread the joy of poetry by sharing at a school assembly or parents day. Oh, and be sure that you, the teacher, memorize and recite a poem, too! Why not use the occasion to memorize a special poem a previous student has written, your own favorite childhood poem, or one that you wrote yourself!

Writing Activity 27 — Seasonal Poetry

> The aim of this activity is to build poetry writing skills.

Use the seasons as a theme to bring poetry into your classroom. The following books have poems related to seasons or weather. Display these and other books in your classroom. Share the poems with your students throughout the day. Then follow up by inviting your students to decide on their favorite season. Write a poem about it.

- *Sky Words,* by Marilyn Singer.
- *A Winter's Yarn,* by Kathleen Cook Waldron.
- *Make Things Fly, Poems about the Wind*, selected by Dorothy M. Kennedy.
- "A Season," by Lillian M. Fisher. From: *More Surprises*, selected by Lee Bennett Hopkins.
- "No," by William Cole. From: *More Surprises*, selected by Lee Bennett Hopkins.
- "I Do Not Mind You, Winter Wind," by Jack Prelutsky. From: *More Surprises*, selected by Lee Bennett Hopkins.
- "Signs of Seasons," by Anonymous. From: *More Surprises*, selected by Lee Bennett Hopkins.
- "Winter Weather," by Margriet Ruurs. From: *Virtual Maniac.*
- *In for Winter, Out for Spring*, by Arnold Adoff.
- *July is a Mad Mosquito*, by J. Patrick Lewis.
- *Snow, Snow: Winter Poems for Children*, by Jane Yolen
- *Under the Cherry Tree*, by Satomi Ichikawa and Cynthia Mitchell.
- *A Circle of Seasons*, by Myra Cohn Livingston.

Seasonal celebrations such as Christmas or Hanukkah can also be used to read and write poetry. Read published poems and use each celebration to create your own classroom poems. Here are some examples to share with your students:

Celebrations, by Myra Cohn Livingston.

Halloween

- *Catmagic*, by Loris Lesynski.
- "Mother Goblin's Lullaby," by Jack Prelutsky. From: *Something Big Has Been Here*.
- *Scared Silly! A Book for the Brave*, by Marc Brown.
- *Best Witches, Poems for Halloween*, by Jane Yolen.
- *Halloween Poems*, by Myra Cohn Livingston.
- *Halloween Stories & Poems*, by Carolyn Feller Bauer.
- "Whose Boo Is Whose?", by X. J. Kennedy. From: *For Laughing Out Loud*, selected by Jack Prelutsky.
- "Witch Goes Shopping," by Lilian Moore. From: *For Laughing Out Loud*, selected by Jack Prelutsky.

Christmas

- *The Night Before Christmas*, by Clement Clarke Moore.
- *Christmas Poems,* by Myra Cohn Livingston.

Perform your own student-written poems during your school assembly.

Valentine's Day

- *Valentine's Day: Stories and Poems,* by Carolyn Feller Bauer.

Send home students' own poems as Valentine cards.

Writing Activity 28 — Whose Viewpoint?

> The aim of this activity is to create awareness
> of different points of view in writing.

Writing an existing story or poem from a different viewpoint can
shed a whole new light on the story line. Look at the following
poem:

School Sick

I don't want to go to school today.
I think I'll be sick so I can stay
in my bed, cozy and warm.
I don't want to go out in rain and storm.
I'll throw up all over the rug
and crawl back to bed, comfy 'n snug.

I'll fake a sore throat and a fever.
My mom is smart but I can deceive her!
I'll have funny lumps with a rash
so she'll want me back in bed in a flash.
That way I can stay home and play,
slumber and snooze the entire day.

Uh oh!
Here comes my mom with bottles and a pill,
she takes my temperature, I have to lie very still!
I don't want to swallow that!
I just may have to get out of bed!
The medicine has a terrible smell,
And all of a sudden I feel very well!

(Margriet Ruurs, *Virtual Maniac*)

Ask your students: Whose viewpoint are we hearing?

How would the story line be different if we heard the same thing
from his mother's point of view. Or the teacher's point of view?
Or who else could we use? Is there perhaps a mouse under the bed,

listening in? Is there a little sister? What about writing the story from the medicine bottle's point of view?!

Try rewriting a poem in a different viewpoint with a variety of poems, such as:

- "My Dog Is Too Friendly," by Bruce Lansky. From: *Poetry Party*. Can you write it from the dog's point of view?
- "The Black Bear," by Jack Prelutsky. From: *Bear in Mind, A Book of Bear Poems*. Can you write it from the bear's point of view?

Writing Activity 29 — Adding Rhyme to Reason

> The aim of this activity is to make poetry a cross-curricular skill.

Add some spice to math lessons by sprinkling it with poetry. You can rap multiplication tables. Instead of just saying them, rap them. Clap the tune or stamp your feet and fall into a rap rhythm:

- Ten - times - four
- Ten - ten - ten - times - four - four - four is
- pff-ahh-pff-ahh-ahh
- for-ty - for-ty.

Use poetry books with a math theme like the ones listed below. Read them with your students and let them inspire you to write your own math poems. Your students could write about selling a toy and what they would do with the money. Or they can write a poem about saving pennies and counting them. Or how about a poem in which they count books in the library? In Sheree Fitch's book, *Sleeping Dragons All Around,* you will encounter Pythagorus, the mathematical dragon. Use him as an example of writing math poetry.

These books and poems will help you on the way to adding rhythm to math:

- "The Monkey" and "Allison Beals and Her 25 Eels," by Shel Silverstein. From: *Falling Up.*
- "I Pulled An 'A' in Math," by Gordon Korman and Bernice Korman. From: *The D- Poems of Jeremy Bloom.*

- *Animal Hours,* by Linda Manning.
- *Math Talk,* by Theoni Pappas.
- *Fractals, Googols and Other Mathematical Tales,* by Theoni Pappas.
- *Adventures of Penrose, the Mathematical Cat*, by Theoni Pappas.
- *A Remainder of One*, by Elinor J. Pinczes.
- The book, *"If You Made a Million,"* by David M. Schwartz, is not rhyming but is lots of fun to use in math and adapts easily for writing their own "Million Poems."

Writing Activity 30 — Take One Line and Add Words

> The aim of this activity is to build poetry writing skills.

Use published books to inspire students' poems. In the school library, find a collection of picture books that have very little text. Some suggested books include:

- *A Mountain Alphabet*, by Margriet Ruurs.
- *A Prairie Alphabet*, by Jo Bannatyne-Cugnet.
- *The Happy Day*, by Marc Simont.
- *When the Wind Stops*, by Charlotte Zolotow.
- *Jessie's Island*, by Sheryl McFarlane.

Ask your students to select one of the books, to read through the different pages, and to then choose one line. That line becomes the first sentence of their poem.

For instance, in *A Mountain Alphabet* I used this sentence for the letter R: *Rambunctious raccoons can be real rascals*. If a student chooses this line, his or her poem might look like the following:

Raccoons

Rambunctious raccoons can be real rascals
The little bandits give me a fright
as they clatter in garbage cans
in the dark alley at the night.

Writing Activity 31 — Personification

> The aim of this activity is to create awareness of personification as a poetry-writing technique.

Explain to your students that "personification" means that we turn an animal or an object into a person by letting them do things that only people can really do. For instance, a bee who is thinking or a house that is waiting. Personification is great to use in poems because it allows us to make a bear laugh or a flower dance. Wordstorm personification possibilities with your students. What kind of traits or actions can they attribute to an animal or an object?

Use these books as examples:

- *There's a Mouse in My House*, by Sheree Fitch.
- "The Dodo," by Peter Wesley-Smith. From: *For Laughing Out Loud*, selected by Jack Prelutsky.

Invite your students to write a personification poem about their favorite animal or object.

The Flower

Have you seen the glory of a flower
that stands proudly over the pond
Staring all day long
at its own reflection?

Have you seen the way
she holds her head in triumph
looking down upon the grass
at how small the blades are
in her shadow?

Have you seen the vainness
in a flower that reflects
in the still waters
that ripple slightly
and then shatter
the flower's image?

(Ashley, Grade 9)

Chapter 3 Bibliography and Web Sites

Bibliography

Adventures of Penrose, the Mathematical Cat, by Theoni Pappas. Wide World Publishing, 1997.

Alligator Pie, by Dennis Lee. Macmillan of Canada, 1974.

A Mountain Alphabet, by Margriet Ruurs. Tundra Books.

Animal Hours, by Linda Manning. Oxford University Press, 1990.

A Prairie Alphabet, by Jo Bannatyne-Cugnet. Tundra Books.

A Remainder of One, by Elinor J. Pinczes. Houghton Mifflin, 1995.

A Royal Pain, by Ellen Conford. New York: Scholastic.

Aska's Animals, by Warabé Aska & David Day. Doubleday, 1991.

Aster Aardvark's Alphabet Adventures, by Steven Kellogg. New York: Morton, 1987.

Awake and Dreaming, by Kit Pearson. Toronto: Puffin Books.

Best Witches, Poems for Halloween, by Jane Yolen. New York: G.P. Putnam's Sons, 1989.

Bear in Mind, A Book of Bear Poems, by Bobbey S. Goldstein. New York: Viking Kestrel, 1989.

Catmagic, by Loris Lesynski. Toronto: Annick Press.

Christmas Poems, by Myra Cohn Livingston. Holiday House, 1988.

A Circle of Seasons, by Myra Cohn Livingston. Holiday House, 1982.

Dinosaurs, by Lee Bennett Hopkins. Orlando, FL: HBJ, 1987.

Falling Up, by Shel Silverstein. HarperCollins, 1996.

For Laughing Out Loud, by Jack Prelutsky. Alfred A. Knopf, 1991.

Fractals, Googols and Other Mathematical Tales, by Theoni Pappas. Wide World Publishing, 1993.

Halloween Poems, by Myra Cohn Livingston. Holiday House, 1989.

Halloween Stories & Poems, by Carolyn Feller Bauer. New York: HarperCollins.

Hatchet, by Gary Paulsen. New York: Puffin Books.

Hoops, by Robert Burleigh. San Diego, CA: Brace, 1997.

If You Made a Million, by David M. Schwartz. Mulberry Books, 1989.

In for Winter, Out for Spring, by Arnold Adoff. Harcourt Brace, 1997.

Jabberwocky, by Lewis Carroll, illustrated by Graeme Base. Harry N. Abrams, 1989.

Jessie's Island, by Sheryl McFarlane. Victoria: Orca Books, B.C.

July is a Mad Mosquito, by J. Patrick Lewis. Atheneum, 1994.

Let Me Be the Boss, by Brod Bagert. Wordsong, Boyds Mills Press, 1992.

Little Red Riding Hood (any version).

Make Things Fly, Poems about the Wind, by Dorothy M. Kennedy. New York: Margaret K. McElderry Books, 1998.

Math Talk, by Theoni Pappas, Wide World Publishing, 1991.

More Surprises, by Lee Bennett Hopkins. New York: Harper & Row.

Owl Moon, by Jane Yolen. New York: Scholastic, 1987.

Poetry Party, by Bruce Lansky. Meadowbrook Press, 1996.

Quiet Storm, Voices of Young Black Poets, compiled by Lydia Okutoro. Hyperion Books, 1999.

Ride A Purple Pelican, by Jack Prelutsky. New York: Greenwillow Books, 1986.

Scared Silly! by Marc Brown. Boston: Little, Brown, and Company, 1994.

Sky Words, by Marilyn Singer. Macmillan Publishing Co., 1994.

Sleeping Dragons All Around, by Sheree Fitch. Toronto: Doubleday Canada, 1989.

Snow, Snow: Winter Poems for Children, by Jane Yolen. Boyds Mills Press, 1998.

Something Big Has Been Here, by Jack Prelutsky. New York: Scholastic, 1992.

Soul Looks Back in Wonder, by Tom Feelings. New York: Dial Books, 1993.

The Complete Nonsense of Edward Lear, by Edward Lear. New York: Dover Publications.

The Cremation of Sam McGee, by Robert Service, illustrated by Ted Harrison. Toronto: Kids Can Press.

The D- Poems of Jeremy Bloom, by Gordon and Bernice Korman, Scholastic, 1992.

The Eleventh Hour, by Graeme Base. Canada: Stoddart, 1988.

The Happy Day, by Marc Simont. New York: Harper & Row.

The Ice Cream Store, by Dennis Lee. HarperCollins, 1991.

The Magic Tree, by David Woolger. Oxford University Press.

The Mitten, by Jan Brett. New York: G. P. Putnam & Sons.

The Night Before Christmas, by Clement Clarke Moore, illustrated by Kim Fernandez. Firefly, 1999.

There's a Mouse in My House, by Sheree Fitch. Toronto: Doubleday Canada, 1997.

The Scholastic Rhyming Dictionary, by Sue Young. New York: Scholastic.

The Sheriff of Rottenshot, by Jack Prelutsky. New York: Greenwillow Books, 1982.

The Sign of the Sea Horse, by Graeme Base. Doublebase Pty Ltd, 1992.

The Whingdingdilly, by Bill Peet. Boston: Houghton Mifflin, 1970.

Toes in My Nose, by Sheree Fitch. Toronto: Doubleday Canada, Ltd.,
    1987.

Two by Two, by Barbara Reid. Toronto: North Winds Press, 1992.

Under the Cherry Tree, by Satomi Ichikawa and Cynthia Mitchell.
    New York: William Collins.

V*alentine's Day: Stories and Poems.,* by Carolyn Feller Bauer.
    HarperCollins, 1993.

Virtual Maniac, by Margriet Ruurs. Gainesville, FL: Maupin House,
    2000.

What's on the Menu?, by Bobbye S. Goldstein. New York: Viking,
    1992.

When the Wind Stops, by Charlotte Zolotow. New York: Harper &
    Row.

Yertle the Turtle, by Dr. Seuss. New York: Random House, 1950.

Useful Web Sites

http://rhyme.lycos.com/ (an on-line rhyming dictionary)

CHAPTER 4

The Editing Process

Now that your students have completed writing several different forms of poetry, look back at the sheets full of poems they have collected in their binders. Having fun with words has allowed them to marvel at language and to *shape* poetry. We now are ready to take that rough piece of wood and do some sanding to make it nice and smooth—to do some editing to make each poem even better.

I would like to make clear what I see as the difference between *editing* and *critiquing*. Critiquing should come first and entails taking a critical look at the overall poem: contents, message, general word use. Does it convey the right image? Editing refers more to grammar, punctuation, and sentence structure.

Critiquing

As students near the completion of a first draft, I make a point of sitting down with each one to critique his or her poem. My main concerns, at this point, are content and mastery of the craft. I ask questions like these:

- Is the writing going the way you wanted it?
- Are you happy with it?
- Does the poem say what you wanted it to say?
- Are your words painting the pictures you see in your head?

Keep in mind that the student should make the decisions that change his or her own writing. All you should do is make (verbal) suggestions and show possible improvement, but the writer should remain in charge of the piece he or she created. Try to guide your students by showing them examples of problems and by making suggestions for change where appropriate. Make suggestions such as:

- How would this sound if. . .
- What if you change this sentence around so you have an easier word to rhyme with?
- Should this be a rhyming poem?

Try to discuss rewriting in a manner that will encourage students rather than overwhelm them. For one student it might be adding a funny ending or finding a different name for a character. Other students can handle more complicated restructuring, such as adding more senses or writing the poem from a different viewpoint.

While you will want to be kind to each author, it is also important that your students grow from your feedback. Telling a student how wonderful his or her poem is will not help improve their next piece of writing. Try to find several positive points to comment on, but also try to give constructive feedback that will help to improve the student's writing. **Concentrate on helping a student to achieve his or her goals. Try not to react personally.** Whether you like the contents is not important. Did the student reach his or her goal of touching the reader, of conveying the message? Did the student use his or her knowledge of craft to create the poem?

Peer Conferencing

Realistically, it is difficult to conference with each student in a class of many! You may want to spread conferencing out over several days or spend a few minutes with each student while the rest of the class is reading. Another way to critique is to team up students and ask them to work together, giving you time to work with individuals. Students can learn to act as effective editors for each other. Discuss criteria beforehand with the entire group. Students reading another student's writing should explain to the writer:

- I liked your poem because. . .
- What I don't like about it is. . .
- You have used alliteration/metaphor/simile and this is what I think about it. . .
- The rhythm, the beat works/is off.

I strongly suggest that the students read the poem out loud because this allows them to hear which lines have too many syllables and which lines need an extra word. This may include substituting a word of two syllables for one with more or fewer syllables. Reading the poem aloud will help to find the right rhythm. Ask them: Does the poem have the right beat? Can you hear that one line is too long? Clap along while you say the poem out loud. Find the right rhythm for each line.

The other students in your class can also serve as a source of inspiration. Encourage your students to talk to each other for ideas and suggestions after plenty of conference modeling. Once a student asked me, "What is a good name for a wizard?" I suggested he ask the group for suggestions and then choose the one he liked best. Great ideas poured forth:

- "Look in *Lord of the Rings*."
- "Spell you own name backwards!"
- "Find a foreign word for wizard," etc.

The suggestions were much more creative than what I would have come up with. Students' suggestions help other students to find new directions for their writing, often giving them renewed energy to write more. But ultimately they are just that—suggestions. The student should be treated as an author in charge of his or her own writing, editing, and rewriting, deciding for himself or herself what to add, where to change something, or which advice to disregard.

The feedback might give the writer good ideas for a complete rewriting of the poem. Or the student might decide to change parts of the poem, shorten a sentence, take out a word, change a line. The writer might also decide that he or she doesn't agree with a particular suggestion and ignore it. Some poems are perfect the first time around. But many do need some "sanding." Once the writer is satisfied with the overall poem, ask him or her to correct spelling (using spell check or dictionary). Correcting punctuation can once again be done through peer conferencing.

At this point, students who are not used to having the freedom to choose their own topics often discover that they really *do* have the power to take their writing in any direction they want. They might ask questions, such as "Can this happen in outer space?" or "Can I make her die at the end?" They delight in the idea that the story line is theirs to take in any direction they chose.

In some cases, kids discover that they were not committed enough to their first idea, that they got bored with it. If that happens, they can look back at their list of ideas and choose a new topic, one with more interesting aspects. Practice makes perfect, right? They thrive with the freedom of choice, even if they now have to work harder to catch up to the first draft writing stage. In the process, even the most reluctant writers surprise themselves by being able to write a strong poem!

All writers need to do many rewrites. Published authors have often had to make changes 50 or 60 times before their text is printed. Publishers may make many suggestions for improvement, but the decision to change the text lies with the author. It may be tedious but it does improve the final product! If you have an author visit coming up, or if you know an author who lives close by, ask the author to bring samples of his or her rewrites. It will show students that we all have to go through this stage.

The editing process should be firmly in the child's hands. This can be difficult sometimes because you may not always agree with the choices your students make. However, I do feel that this is one area in where the students can make their own decisions. Even if we don't like it, it doesn't mean that it's wrong! But making their own decisions during the writing process leads to a strong feeling of ownership, commitment, and pride in their work. Referring to children's ownership of a piece of writing, Dr. Donald Graves, in Lucy McCormick Calkins' case study *Lessons from a Child*, says, "When people own a place, they look after it. When it belongs to someone else, they couldn't care less." Having the freedom to make their own decisions versus completing assigned topics with little or no choice gives the young author ownership in his or her writing.

Here is an example of how drastically a piece of writing can change, and improve, with some guidance. Angela, in grade 9, was writing prose. She told me that she didn't really like writing poetry. When I critiqued her story I told her that her writing was very poetic and suggested she put the sentences in a little bit different format. I showed her, on a sheet of paper, how her story changed when it took the shape of poetry.

This was the prose she had written:

> I remember that night I walked through the door to an
> empty house. I thought I was dreaming but I wasn't. I sat
> there for hours thinking of you, the hours we had, the days
> we spent running. Now you are gone, gone like the wind.
> I went to the door thinking it was you. I remember that
> night, that night without you.

I broke up her sentences and this is the poem that Angela ended up
with after her editing:

That Night

I remember that night
I walked through the door
to an empty house.

I thought I was dreaming,
a nightmare, but it wasn't. . .

I sat there for hours
thinking of you
and the hours we had,
the days we spent running.

Now you are gone,
gone like the wind.

I went to the door
thinking it was you.
I remember that night
that first night without you.

Incidentally, Angela told me the piece of writing was about the day
her dog died. She loved, and was very proud of, the poem she
discovered she had written!

CHAPTER 5

Publishing and Sharing

The Need for an Audience

Writers write so that readers can read. Audience is an essential element of writing. After all, the main purpose of writing is to have someone *read* your writing. The class is fine as audience for a while, but writers get excited about the prospect of new audiences. "Teachers need to struggle to find new audiences for their classes" (Mem Fox, *Radical Reflections*). So when you have been writing poems with your students, you will want to share their accomplishments with others.

After a child goes through all the hard work of producing a good piece of writing, you can prevent them from saying, "Now what?" by offering opportunities to show their writing to the rest of the world. Whether it is publishing in the classroom or publishing on-line, by reading at an assembly, or by sharing with parents, be sure to celebrate the accomplishment. Offer them a real audience!

The Publishing Process

Once you start discussing various ways in which you can publish classroom books, it's a good idea to use the exercise to teach your students how books are published. Use and display the following books in your classroom to explain the process from writing through editing and illustrating to the final printed and bound product:

- *How a Book Is Made*, by Aliki.
- *Write Now!* by Karleen Bradford.
- *Making a Picture Book*, by Anne Bower Ingram.
- *What Do Authors Do?* by Eileen Christelow.
- *Just Write!* by Sylvia Gunnery.
- *From Pictures to Words, A Book about Making a Book*, by Janet Stevens.
- *Writing Your Best Picture Book Ever*, by Kathy Stinson.
- *Writing Picture Books*, by Kathy Stinson.

Designing and Illustrating Books

Once the editing process has been completed, help students produce a book of poems. A book not only showcases the poems but teaches students about the publishing process as well. When I do school visits, students are usually intrigued to learn how books are actually made. Most kids have no idea how books get printed or how they get illustrated. Creating awareness increases their interest. Besides, publishing your own book of poetry is fun! We'll talk here about producing a book on plain white paper that has a laminated cover, a spiral coil binding, and illustrations.

You might want to state some criteria for selecting the poems and deciding the number of poems to be included in the book. First you'll need to decide if you will publish one book for each individual student-poet, or a classroom anthology. (Of course, each student gets a copy.)

When I complete a poetry workshop with students, I generally make one book for each individual student that includes their own poems that have made it through the critiquing and editing process. Each student's book will then include the whole spectrum of poems we have been writing: rhyming, non-rhyming, tongue twisters, poetry written to music, metaphors, and more.

But you might also decide to publish an anthology of selected work from the entire classroom. Your selection criterion might be to include samples of all formats of writing. Ask each student to submit two favorite poems. Be sure to give all students equal exposure.

Fonts

Your students first need to decide whether they want to produce a vertically oriented book (see Figure A), or one oriented horizontally (see Figure B). If the latter, remember to adjust the printer to print in the landscape mode. Also, make any illustrations run this way.

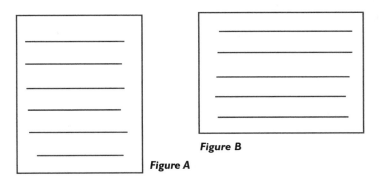

Figure B

Figure A

So, let's make books of poetry in the classroom. First, tell your students to type each poem on the computer and print one poem per sheet of paper. Show them their options: fonts, sizes, spacing, etc. by printing one sample poem on a sheet of paper. The font in which it is printed has an effect on the visual impact of the poem. Let them experiment with different fonts that enhance the contents of the poem, for example, bold, italic, ornate, small, and so on.

Illustrations

Next, you can ask your students to decide what kind of illustrations to make with each poem. Illustrations can be made in color or black and white. Offer an assortment of markers, crayons, coloring pencils, and even paint. Computer graphics might be used or you can use different forms of artwork, like collage, plasticine, or block printing. Combine this activity with any art form that suits your art curriculum. As in the writing process, allow students to plan, draft, and work on their illustrations on separate pieces of paper first.

Because a few children just "hate" doing their own pictures, I like to offer an option to drawing their own illustrations by supplying them with a huge pile of book publishers' catalogues from which they can cut and paste illustrations and decorations. These catalogues have wonderful artwork. Book catalogues usually come out twice a year, in the spring and fall. Ask for them at any bookstore. They will gladly supply you with last season's catalogues.

You can give students the freedom to choose *not* to illustrate their books. Most professional authors do not illustrate their own work. "Real writers who can't paint don't illustrate their own stories. Kids who don't like drawing should not be made to illustrate their own writing" (Mem Fox, *Radical Reflections*). Many children, and adults, too, are surprised to learn that authors and illustrators do not necessarily work together at all. When a text is accepted for publication by a publisher, it becomes the publisher's responsibility to assign it to an illustrator. Two of my picture books have been illustrated by a wonderful illustrator whom I had never met. I never even talked to her on the phone. We finally met three years after the first book came out. In fact, while she was working on the illustrations, our publisher did not want us talking to each other!

You also may want to offer your students the option of having their writing illustrated by someone else. Why not let the kids ask someone in their class or in the school to illustrate their book? They may have a brother who's very good at drawing or a friend who'd love to help out. Be sure to include the illustrator's name on the cover.

Covers

Students are now busy creating their illustrations, finishing the final drafts, or typing their stories on the computer. It's not a bad idea at this time to discuss covers for their books. Have a collection of books from the library on hand to show different covers. Choose some with attractive covers, some with what you consider to be boring covers. Try to find a variety of fonts and colors.

Discuss with your students:

- What makes a cover attractive?
- What kind of illustration is on the cover?
- What does it tell you about the contents of the book?
- How big are the letters for title and author/illustrator names?

Ask your students to think about an attractive cover design.
Do they have a catchy, attractive title for their poetry collection?
It could be the name of one of the poems or any fun title.
Alliterations sometimes work well for a book title.

Ask students to design a cover for their own books, complete with
an illustration, a title, and the author's name. If you decide on an
authology, several students can work together to create the cover.
Covers can be mounted on colored construction paper and then
laminated.

To learn more about the publishing process, stop by your local
newspaper or large printing business and ask for:

- samples of pages before they get cut (books and newspapers are
  not printed page by page but on huge sheets of paper).

- color separations, to show students how books are printed in
  only four colors: yellow, blue, red, and black. Look at any
  picture book or magazine with a magnifying glass to discover
  that all pictures are made up of dots of these four colors!

Most newspaper publishers use these items and throw them out
after use. They make great classroom props. Even more fun:
arrange for a field trip with your class to a local newspaper or book
printer so your students can see the entire publishing process.

About the Author

When producing books in the classroom, encourage your authors to
write a page, "About the Author." This can include a short bio-
graphical write-up as well as a photo. For examples refer to bios on
book jackets in the library. A photo can be pasted on a sheet of
paper or you can use a digital camera to print it. Students may also
choose to do a self-portrait. The students should decide whether
they want this page, "About the Author," to be put on the outside of
the back cover or inside the book. A class photograph works well
for the anthology, and students can have fun writing a biography of
their class. Again, giving them that choice makes the process much
more exciting than compelling students to conform to one standard
way of doing the books.

To complete designing the books, students can produce:

- a **title page**, showing just the title and the author's name in a font
  of their choice.

- a **dedication page**, which can be to their best friend, their parents, or even to their dog!

- an **index**, if applicable.

- Some students may want to write a **short contents** to paste on the back cover of their book, complete with an excerpt from one poem.

- They may even want to write a fictional **review**! "Ten weeks on the New York Bestsellers List!"

- **ISBN**: every book in the world has its own ISBN (International Standard Book Number). ISBNs for the students' poetry books may be composed of birth dates, phone numbers, or secret codes.

- Students can learn about **copyright** by writing their own copyright page complete with the standard copyright warning and symbol. Look inside any book for an example of the text, author name, dates and copyright symbol. (Most computer keypads have the © under "option—g.") Use this activity to discuss how copyright protects an author's work.

Assembling the Books

Give your students a file folder or large envelope to store their finished work. Make a checklist like this one for your students to help them complete the publishing process:

Name: _____

- ☑ Check each item as you complete it. Keep your finished pages clean and flat!
- ☐ Make a cover, with title and author's name
- ☐ Print a dedication page
- ☐ Make several large illustrations for inside your book
- ☐ Print title page (just the title and your name)
- ☐ Print © page
- ☐ Print your poems, double-spaced, on numbered pages
- ☐ Print Table of Contents (optional)
- ☐ Print page "About the Author" with a photo

When everything is finished, pages should be carefully assembled. Ask each student to make sure pages are in the right order and right-side-up! Now the book is ready to be bound! To bind the books I like using a plastic coil binding. Most schools have a binding machine tucked away somewhere, but chances are that the students have never been allowed to use one. They'll find it fascinating to see how it works. If your school does not have one of these machines, an office supply store can attach coil bindings for you for a small fee.

Make use of volunteer parents when you are ready to assemble and bind books.

Other options to bind the books include using yarn, large staples, or a binder. You can also use a clear plastic cover with a spine that slides over the pages. Even a new (illustrated!) duotang can give a polished look to students' writing. You can also purchase ready-made blank books in which your students can write or paste poems and illustrations. The cover of a blank book can be colored and personalized.

Book Launch

Parents

Try to involve the parents with the writing activities as much as possible. This will also help to ensure their support of the child at home in reading and writing activities.

The crucial role of parents is confirmed by John Spink in his book *Children as Readers*: "Parents have a central role to play in helping children to become competent readers. The partnership between teachers, parents and children in reading programs has proved to be very successful—a mutually rewarding process involving encouragement of private reading as well as public reading, book sharing and book ownership."

When parents participate, the children will write in an atmosphere of greater support. When parents are part of the child's writing process, they become more aware of the different skills learned by the child while he or she is writing and rewriting and, usually, more supportive of you because they have an understanding of what goes on in the classroom.

Because many parents work during the day and are unable to come to school, consider having the book launch during the lunch hour or in the evening. A special event often makes the students feel that their work is even more important and appreciated.

Planning the Book Launch

Celebrate your students' achievements by throwing a party! All the writing, rewriting, word processing, illustrating, and binding have culminated into one big event: a book launch! Invite parents, grandparents, and siblings. Why not include your principal, district's superintendent, school board members, or other special people who'd enjoy hearing your students' accomplishments. Another classroom could also be invited. You and your students should be proud of your accomplishments and might as well show off!

Invitations

Carefully consider the best time for the party and discuss it with your students. Ask some students to design an invitation on the computer. Someone else might contribute an illustration while yet two other students decide on the text. Be sure to include time, date, and place. You might want to ask parents to contribute to the fun by bringing cookies or juice. You may even want to design a rhyming invitation!

Prep Time

Before the event, explain that a book launch introduces a new book to readers. Encourage them to think about what they want to share about their own book of poetry. Tell your students you'd like them to talk to the audience about what gave them the idea to write these poems and to choose one or two of their favorite poems to read aloud.

If you have students who absolutely dread the idea of standing up in front of others to share, please don't force them. If anyone is truly uncomfortable, assure him or her that you won't call on that student but that, during the party, you can hold up that author's book and briefly mention some of its highlights. Once they see how well the others are received, they may lose their anxiety and decide to present their own writing!

During the book launch, the authors take turns speaking about their books and giving sample readings for the visitors. Many parents will have observed the child at home working on the book as he or she was engaged in the writing, but for others this will be the first time they hear some of the writing. In almost all instances, parents will be amazed at their child's ability to write and the wide variety of books produced.

I have invited a local news reporter to several book launches to take photos of the students and to interview the young authors. Having students' pictures in the paper because they wrote poems helps to generate excitement for writing. The entire writing process goes hand in hand with increased confidence and self-esteem.

"Producing a finished product gives us not only the satisfaction of making something others can enjoy, but also, knowledge of the process. Children can learn a tremendous amount about how literature works by producing some" (Perry Nodelman, *The Pleasures of Children's Literature*).

At the conclusion of the readings, invite the audience to leaf through the displayed books and to visit with the authors. As a follow-up, you may also consider asking the students to read from their books during a school assembly.

More Ideas on Publishing in the Classroom

- Produce books of poetry as a joint project with primary buddies. Your students can write for a younger audience. The younger children can add the illustrations.

- Poems and illustrations can be published on the computer in HyperCard as an animated picture book.

- If poems are written by one person and illustrated by someone else, produce two copies. Show name of author and illustrator on the cover.

- A second copy of the book can be made for the school library, complete with bar code.

Other Ways to Share and Celebrate

- To display poetry written by students, try a Poet Tree. Draw a huge tree with branches on a large sheet of brown or green paper. Cut out and tape to a wall in the school hallway or classroom. The students can write poems on leaf-shaped paper. (I use maple leaf-shaped note pads from educational supply stores.) Children can also spread one hand on a sheet of colored paper, trace it, and cut it out. Tape leaves with poems all over the tree. Poets sign the branches of their Poet Tree.

- Cut strips from colored construction paper. Ask students to write the title and author of each book or poem that they read, on a strip of paper. Link pieces of paper together until you have a garland decoration for the classroom.

- Publish some of the poems in a school newsletter or submit them to your local community newspaper. Find out about Newspapers in Education and how you can make use of this national program. (http://www.naa.org/foundation/)

- Invite each student to submit his or her best poem to you, as the "publisher" and bind the collection into an anthology for classroom or school use. Knowing that you will keep and treasure their writing will make them feel honored.

- Use special occasions such as Children's Book Week or April 2, International Children's Book Week, to celebrate children's writing.

- Have students share their poetry by reciting it at a local seniors' home. Or contact your local radio station and discuss ways to have students read their writing on the air.

- Share outstanding poems by publishing them on your school's Web site, on a page of "Students' Writing." Illustrations can be scanned and posted as well.

Submitting Poetry to Magazines

When you do have some outstanding poems, you can encourage your students to try to publish them in a magazine. Submitting writing to a magazine can be a time-consuming process and frustrating. But it is also enormously rewarding to see the poem in print!

This is how students should prepare:

- Decide which magazine is most suited for your poem. The editorial address will be inside.

- Send edited writing on clean, white paper and double space it. Always include a S.A.S.E.—a self-addressed stamped envelope, with any writing you send to a publisher. Use an envelope that your writing will fit in, buy an extra stamp that covers the cost to return it, and put it in with your story. If you live in the United States and you want to send your writing to Canada, you will need to have some Canadians stamps (and vice versa). Ask a relative or friend who is visiting or who lives in the country, to bring some back for you.

- Write a cover letter to explain who you are and why you hope they will publish your poem.

Magazines sometimes don't pay anything and sometimes they pay quite well ($75 for a short poem). If magazines want your story or poem, they will usually write you a letter and include a contract. They send you a check and a copy of the magazine once they publish your work. Once you start submitting your writing to book publishers or to magazines, prepare yourself for rejections. Every writer gets them! Dr. Seuss had his first book rejected 27 times! But Gordon Korman had his first book accepted for publication when he was in seventh grade!

Magazines That Publish Writing by Children

Please note that this is not an all-inclusive list.

- *OWL* and *Chickadee*
  56 The Esplanade, Suite 304
  Toronto, Ontario M5E 1A7, Canada

- *Potluck*
  Box 546
  Deerfield, IL 60015-0546
  or http://members.aol.com/_ht_a/nappic/index.html

- *Kidsworld Magazine*
  345 Danforth Ave.
  Toronto, Ontario M4K 1N7, Canada
  or http://www.kidsworld-online.com/

- *Highlights For Children* ("Our Own Pages")
  803 Church Street
  Honesdale, PA 18431
- *Stone Soup,* a magazine by and for children under 13
  Editor
  P.O. Box 83
  Santa Cruz, CA 95063
  or http://www.stonesoup.com/

See also the list of writing sites on the Internet at the end of this chapter.

Publishing on the Internet

Another way to give your students an audience is by making use of the World Wide Web! It is already there, waiting for you to share. In most cases, it's free. And it's a lot faster and easier than publishing in print. School Web sites can be used to post students' poetry.

Sometimes parents and teachers are hesitant to use the Internet, fearing that children won't read books when they use technology. But when children spend time word processing, they are reading and writing. When children communicate by e-mail with others around the world, they are reading and writing for a real purpose. When children find information on the Web, they read. When a student posts a message that can be read by thousands, he or she is conscious of spelling and makes sure that it is done correctly.

In fact, it has been said that the art of letter writing, as well as the ancient tradition of storytelling, is making a comeback through technology. Computers offer these opportunities.

Computers never could, or should replace a teacher as mentor or act as a substitute for human dialogue in guiding students. Test results, however show that a hands-on approach with computers is an extraordinarily rich means of learning, across a wide range of cognitive and behavioral styles. In fact, many children said to have been disabled flourish in a hands-on environment. (Reluctant to try computer technology? Read *The Connected Family: Bridging the Digital Generation Gap*, by Seymour Papert.)

Integrating technology into classroom practices uses these valuable resources in a more effective manner and offers alternative learning styles to children. Find ways to make computer lab time relevant and authentic by giving students writing activities to follow up on from the classroom.

By using word processors and printers, children can make their books look good. They can print covers and title pages, scan a photo of the author, and put a real copyright symbol on their work.

Using e-mail to teach writing gives a student both the use of a word processor and the use of the Internet to connect with a professional to consult. Not only do students benefit from this form of communication, but e-mail allows me, as a mentor, to work and connect with children when it suits me rather than having to be in a classroom at a set time. It also allows the child to write independently and in privacy, away from peers who might influence the child if writing was done as a shared classroom activity.

I created an e-mail writing program after I visited a seventh-grade class in a school in a small community. After writing poetry all afternoon, a big, burly seventh grader in a leather jacket sauntered over to me, handed me a crumpled up piece of paper, and mumbled, "Don't look at it until you've left." Which I did. Then I found a beautiful, sensitive poem and realized this is the kind of writer I wanted to reach. A student who doesn't want his peers to know he enjoys, but who really likes, and grows from, writing. E-mail allows me to reach these kids.

Connecting with an Audience

An on-line magazine, or e-zine, in which children can see their writing published, allows for a faster turnover of contents and is much less costly to produce than a printed magazine. An e-zine allows students to share their writing easily with an audience around the world and offers an opportunity to read writing by peers. Other children can comment, give feedback, get ideas for their own writing and generally help a young author to grow as a writer and as a reader. Children anywhere can read each other's stories, generate ideas, use their imaginations, and improve their vocabulary and spelling while doing so. Reading and writing will be done with a real purpose.

Publishing an E-Zine

A simple computer with modem, and space on a server are all that you need to create your own Web magazine. If your school already has its own Web site you may choose to use this as the place to post your students' writing. Ask your school's technology coordinator for help.

If you are going to post your students' stories on the Internet, here are some recommendations:

- Offer an opportunity to publish and to read writing by kids.
- Focus on writing.
- Make it a simple, easy-to-use Web site.
- Add hot links to related sites.
- Use stories and poems and perhaps illustrations.
- Publish only the student-poet's first name.
- Obtain parental consent if needed, or make sure that the posted personal information complies with the rules in your school or district.
- Use a limited number of graphics so download time is fast.

Most word processing programs allow you to post stories directly in HTML language. The technology coordinator should also be able to assist you in creating the Web pages if you need help. If no technology consultant is available, try a high-school student! Sometimes they can help you with all of your problems and earn credit at the same time.

The first page on a Web site, the Home Page, is usually an introduction to the school with links to related pages of information. You can create a new link with a button that says something like "Students' Poems" or "Our Published Pages." When readers click on this button it will take them to the pages of stories that your children have created.

Type the children's writing on your computer, or simply transfer it onto your computer from their disks, and then "upload" the files to the server. You can use any kind of Web page software for this purpose.

I have posted writing on the Internet by children who participated in writing workshops that I conducted in different schools. After their stories and poems were posted, students and teachers visited the Web site to critique its usability and contents. I discussed the on-line magazine's relevancy, practical use, contents, etc. with children because I wanted to find out how the student viewed the site in relation to his or her own writing. Students participating in these discussions came from Grades 4 to 8.

Their feedback is interesting. When discussing how the use of this Web site would relate to their own writing, students' comments included the following:

- I liked knowing that some of the poems were read by people locally and others were from far away.

- It helped me to get ideas from reading other students' writing.

- Reading other children's writing shows how different everyone writes. It's fun!

- I liked to see what ideas other children had used.

Most students felt that reading the e-zine would be helpful to their own writing, both in reading other people's writing and in getting ideas. Most felt that knowing a Web site was available would encourage them to write more. Invariably, students commented that they enjoyed reading other students' writing. They commented on the value of seeing their writing published:

- Sometimes I read someone else's poem and it inspires me to write my own. Reading [a site like this] encourages me to write more.

- If the poem I wrote was really good, I would want to submit it to be published on a Web site. Knowing that your story or poem was to be published would be exciting.

- I would love to publish a poem to show other children that I can write, too.

- It's much easier to read an online magazine than having to buy one.

- It is too cumbersome to submit writing to a regular magazine, having to get an envelope and postage, etc.

All students felt that friends, parents and relatives would want to read their writing once it was published on-line.

I was surprised that none of the children mentioned that being published on-line would somehow be less impressive than to have writing published in a printed magazine. When no one raised this issue, I eventually asked the children if they felt it to be less "real" to be published on the Internet as compared to being published in a printed magazine. The children strongly disagreed, saying that it would be much better to be published on-line "because then everyone can read it."

Using computers and connectivity allows students to develop skills necessary in other areas of their education as well as in their future endeavors. Perhaps we can apply the enthusiasm children show for computer and video games and help them to direct it towards writing. By having a place to post and share their writing, children will write more, enjoy doing so, and be proud of their accomplishments.

Chapter 5 Bibliography and Web Sites

Bibliography

Children as Readers, by John Spink. London: Clive Bingley, 1989.
From Pictures to Words, A Book About Making a Book, by Janet Stevens. New York: Holiday House.
How a Book Is Made, by Aliki. New York: Harper Trophy.
Just Write! by Sylvia Gunnery. Canada: Pembroke Publishers.
Making a Picture Book, by Anne Bower Ingram. Australia: Methuen.
Radical Reflections: Passionate Opinions on Teaching, Learning and Living, by Mem Fox. Harcourt, Brace & Company, 1993.
The Connected Family, Bridging the Digital Generation Gap, by Seymour Papert. Atlanta: Longstreet Press.
The Pleasures of Children's Literature, by Perry Nodelman. Longman, 1992.
What Do Authors Do? by Eileen Christelow. New York: Clarion Books.
Write Now! by Karleen Bradford. Canada: Scholastic.
Writing Picture Books, by Kathy Stinson. Canada: Pembroke.
Writing Your Best Picture Book Ever, by Kathy Stinson. Canada: Pembroke.

On-Line Writing Sites for Kids

http://rhyme.lycos.com/

http://www-dept.usm.edu/~connect/connec.html

http://www.chebucto.ns.ca/~greebie/Criticism/contents.html

http://www.inkspot.com/young/

http://mgfx.com/kidlit/

http://www.inform.umd.edu/UMS+State/MDK12_Stuff/homepers/emag

http://www.candlelightstories.com/

http://www.ala.org/parentspage/greatsites/lit.html

http://www.stonesoup.com

http://www.kidpub.org/kidpub/

http://www.cyberkids.com/index.html

On-Line Writing Resources for Educators

http://falcon.jmu.edu/~ramseyil/writing.htm

http://www.users.interport.net/~hdu/

http://www.acs.ucalgary.ca/~dkbrown/writings.html

http://www.ala.org/parentspage/greatsites/parent.html

http://www3.sympatico.ca/ccbc/

http://www.bookadventure.org/

http://www.reading.org/about/

http://www.naa.org/foundation/

http://www.usatoday.com/news/nweird.htm

http://rhyme./lycos.com

http://www.ibby.org

http://www.hbook.com

After Words

Classroom Poems

I live in fear
that I
will teach the poem
and they
will lose the poet
and the song
and the self
within the poem.

I live in fear
that I
who love the poem
and the children
will lose the poem
and the children
when I teach the poem.

But I will teach the poem
Live with the fear
Love the children
Sing the song
Find the self
And know the poet
is beside me
Just as afraid
But full of hope.

(David Booth, *Poems Please*)

It's my hope that this book has helped you find some new activities, some new ways in which to help your students discover, first and foremost, the *joy* of writing poetry. I hope it wasn't a one-time experience and that you will keep writing and using poetry throughout your day, every day of your teaching.

Whether you publish the poems or post them on the Internet, share them other students or parents, I hope you will instill a lifelong love of poetry in your students.

I suggest that you join your state or provincial IRA, the International Reading Association, to discover more great literature and to meet writers at annual conferences. But most of all, savor poetry each and every day!

Treasure Chest

Open the cover of the book in your hands,
bridge to unknown and wonderful lands.
Travel through countries of wisdom and fun,
nights full of darkness, days full of sun.

Turn each page full of wonder,
follow its road to up yonder
where mountain tops talk to the sky
whispering a wondering 'why'?

Treasure chest of make-believe places,
meeting new and familiar faces.
Reach for a book on the shelf—
Discover the world, discover yourself.

(Margriet Ruurs)

Bibliography

NOTE: I have tried to make it easier for you to find books for your particular grade level by marking some books

P = mostly for use with primary students

I = mostly for use with intermediate students

+ = this book is particularly good to use with older, high school students

ESL = particularly good to use with ESL students

Books without a mark appeal to all ages

Recommended Books of Poetry

Adoff, Arnold. *Black Is Brown Is Tan.* HarperCollins, 1987.

Adoff, Arnold. *In for Winter, Out for Spring.* Harcourt Brace, 1997.

Adoff, Arnold. *Outside Inside Poems.* Voyager Picture Books, 1995.

Ahlberg, Janet, & Allan Ahlberg. *The Jolly Postman.* London: Heinemann, 1986.

Bagert, Brod. *Chicken Socks: and Other Contagious Poems.* Boyds Mills Press, 2000.

Bagert, Brod. *Let Me Be the Boss.* Wordsong, Boyds Mills Press, 1992.

Bagert, Brod. *Rainbows, Head Lice and Pea Green Tile: Poems in the Voice of the Classroom Teacher.* Gainesville, FL.: Maupin House, 1999.

Base, Graeme. *Animalia.* Willowisp Press, 1986.

Base, Graeme. *The Eleventh Hour.* Stoddart, Canada, 1988. **I**

Base, Graeme. *Jabberwocky*, by Lewis Carroll. Harry N. Abrams. 1989

Base, Graeme. *Sign of the Seahorse.* Doublebase Pty., 1992. **+**

Base, Graeme. *The Worst Band in the Universe.* Toronto: Doubleday Canada, 1999. **+**

Bell Mathis, Sharon. *Red Dog Blue Fly, Football Poems.* Viking, New York. **I/+**

Bennett Hopkins, Lee, compiler. *Dinosaurs.* Orlando: HBJ, 1987.

Bennett Hopkins, Lee. *Extra Innings: Baseball Poems.* Harcourt Brace, 1993.

Bennett Hopkins, Lee. *More Surprises.* Harper & Row, New York.

Brown, Marc. *Scared Silly! A Book for the Brave.* Boston: Little, Brown, 1994.

Bryant, Ashley. *Ashley Bryan's ABC of African American Poetry.* Atheneum, 1997.

Burleigh, Robert. *Hoops.* San Diego, Calif.: Harcourt, Brace, 1997. **+**

Candlewick Book of First Rhymes. Cambridge, Mass.: Candlewick Press, 1996. **ESL**

Clarke Moore, Clement. *The Night before Christmas*, illustrated by Kim Fernandez. Firefly, 1999.

Cohn Livingston, Myra. *Celebrations.* Holiday House, 1985.

Cohn Livingston, Myra. *Christmas Poems.* Holiday House, 1988.

Cohn Livingston, Myra. *A Circle of Seasons.* Holiday House, 1982.

Cohn Livingston, Myra. *Easter Poems.* Holiday House, 1989.

Cohn Livingston, Myra. *Halloween Poems.* Holiday House, 1989.

Cook Waldron, Kathleen. *A Winter's Yarn.* Red Deer College Press, 1986.

Dahl, Roald. *Revolting Rhymes.* London: Puffin Books, 1982. **+**

Day, David. *Aska's Animals,* illustrated by Warabé Aska. Doubleday, 1991. **+**

Feelings, Tom. *Daydreamers.* E. P. Dutton, 1993.

Feelings, Tom. *Soul Looks back in Wonder.* New York: Dial Books, 1993. **+**

Feller Bauer, Caroline. *Halloween Stories and Poems*. HarperCollins, New York.

Feller Bauer, Caroline. *Valentine's Day: Stories and Poems*. New York: HarperCollins, 1993.

Fitch, Sheree. *If You Could Wear My Sneakers*. Toronto: Doubleday Canada, 1997.

Fitch, Sheree. *Sleeping Dragons All Around*. Toronto: Doubleday Canada, 1989.

Fitch, Sheree. *There Are Monkeys in My Kitchen*. Toronto: Doubleday Canada, 1992.

Fitch, Sheree. *There's a Mouse in My House*. Toronto: Doubleday Canada, 1997.

Fitch, Sheree. *Toes in My Nose and Other Poems*. Toronto: Doubleday Canada, 1987.

Goldstein, Bobbye S. *Bear In Mind, A Book of Bear Poems*. Viking Kestrel, New York, 1989.

Goldstein, Bobbye S. compiler. *What's on the Menu?* New York: Viking, 1992.

Harley, Avis. *Fly with Poetry: An ABC of Poetry*. Boyds Mill Press, 2000.

Huigin, Sean O. *Ghost Horse of the Mounties*. Toronto: Black Moss Press, 1983.

Huigin, Sean O. *I'll Belly Your Button in a Minute*. Toronto: Black Moss Press, 1985.

Huigin, Sean O. *Pickles and the Dog Nappers*. Toronto: Black Moss Press, 1986.

Ichikawa, Satomi. *Under the Cherry Tree*, written by Cynthia Mitchell. William Collins, New York.

Katz, Bobbi. *Truck Talk, Rhymes on Wheels*. New York: Scholastic, 1997.

Kellogg, Steven. *Aster Aardvark's Alphabet Adventures*. New York: Morton, 1987.

Kellogg, Steven. *There Was an Old Woman*. New York: Four Winds Press.

Kennedy, Dorothy M., editor. *Make Things Fly*. New York: Margaret K. McElderry Books, 1998.

Korman, Gordon, with Bernice Korman. *The D- Poems of Jeremy Bloom*. New York: Scholastic, 1992.   **I**

Korman, Gordon, with Bernice Korman. *The Last Place Sports Poems of Jeremy Bloom*. New York: Scholastic, 1996.   **I**

Lansky, Bruce. *A Bad Case of the Giggles: Kid's Favorite Funny Poems*. Meadowbrook Press, 1994.

Lansky, Bruce. *Poetry Party*. Meadowbrook Press, 1996.

Lear, Edward. *The Complete Nonsense of Edward Lear*. Dover, New York.

Lee, Dennis. *Alligator Pie*. Macmillan of Canada, 1974.

Lee, Dennis. *Garbage Delight*. Macmillan of Canada, 1979.

Lee, Dennis. *Jelly Belly*. Macmillan of Canada, 1983.

Lee, Dennis. *The Ice Cream Store*. HarperCollins, 1991.

Lesynski, Lois. *Catmagic*. Annick Press, Toronto.

Lewis, J. Patrick. *The Bookworm's Feast: A Potluck of Poems*. Dial Books, 1999.

Lewis, J. Patrick. *July is a Mad Mosquito*. Atheneum, 1994.

Little, Jean. *I Know an Old Laddie*. Viking, Toronto.

Martin, Bill, Jr., with John Archambault. *Barn Dance*. New York: Henry Holt, 1986.

Omolola Okutoro, Lydia. *Quiet Storm, Voices of Young Black Poets*. Hyperion Books, 1999.   **+**

Peet, Bill. *Huge Harold*. Boston: Houghton Mifflin, 1961.

Peet, Bill. *The Whingdingdilly*. Boston: Houghton Mifflin, 1970.

Pomerantz, Charlotte. *If I Had a Paka*. New York: Greenwillow Books.

Prelutsky, Jack. *For Laughing Out Loud*. Alfred A. Knopf, 1991.

Prelutsky, Jack. *A Pizza the Size of the Sun*. Greenwillow Books, New York

Prelutsky, Jack. *Ride a Purple Pelican*. New York: Greenwillow
Prelutsky, Jack. Books, 1986.   **P**

Prelutsky, Jack. *Ride a Purple Pelican*, taped edition. Music by Michael Isaacson, Listening Library, 1988.   **P**

Prelutsky, Jack. *The Sheriff of Rottenshot*. New York: Greenwillow Books, 1982.

Prelutsky, Jack. *Something Big Has Been Here*. New York: Scholastic, 1992.

Prelutsky, Jack. *Tyrannosaurus Was a Beast*. New York: Greenwillow Books, 1988.

Prelutsky, Jack, and Dr. Seuss. *Hooray For Diffendoofer Day!* New York: Alfred A. Knopf, 1998.   I

Reid, Barbara. *Two By Two*. Toronto: North Winds Press, 1992.

Reid, Barbara. *The Party*. Canada: Scholastic, 1997.

Service, Robert. *The Best of Robert Service*. Toronto: McGraw Hill Ryerson.   +

Service, Robert. *The Cremation of Sam McGee*, illustrated by Ted Harrison. Kids Can Press, Toronto.

Service, Robert. *The Shooting of Dan McGrew*, illustrated by Ted Harrison. Kids Can Press, Toronto.

Seuss, Dr., and Jack Prelutsky. *Hooray for Diffendoofer Day!* New York: Alfred A. Knopf, 1998.

Seuss, Dr. *I Can Read With My Eyes Shut*. New York: Random House.

Seuss, Dr. *Oh, the Places You'll Go*. New York: Random House, 1990.   I

Seuss, Dr. *Yertle the Turtle*. New York: Random House, 1950.

Silverstein, Shel. *Falling Up*. New York: HarperCollins, 1996.

Singer, Marilyn. *Sky Words*. Macmillan, 1994.

Viorst, Judith. *The Alphabet from Z to A: (With Much Confusion on the Way)*. Atheneum, 1994.

Woolger, David. *The Magic Tree, Poems of Fantasy and Mystery*. Oxford University Press, 1981.   +

Yolen, Jane. *Alphabestiary: Animal Poems from A to Z*. Boyds Mills Press, 1995.

Yolen, Jane. *Best Witches, Poems for Halloween*. New York: G. P. Putnam's Sons, 1989.

Yolen, Jane. *Mouse's Birthday*. New York: G. P. Putnam's Sons, 1993.   P

Yolen, Jane. *Owl Moon*. New York: Scholastic, 1987.

Yolen, Jane. *Sea Watch*. New York: Philomel Books.   +

Yolen, Jane. *Snow, Snow: Winter Poems for Children.* Boyds Mills Press, 1998.

Yolen, Jane. *Street Rhymes Around the World.* Boyds Mills Press, 1992

Yolen, Jane. *Color Me a Rhyme, Nature Poems for Young People.* Boyds Mills Press, 2000.

Other Relevant Books

A Child's Garden of Verses, by Robert Louis Stevenson. Oxford University Press, 1966.

Oh, the Places He Went, by Maryann N. Weidt. Minneapolis, Minn.: Carolrhoda Books, 1994.

The Bat Poet, by Randall Jarrell, illustrated by Maurice Sendak. HarperCollins, 1996.

The Complete Nonsense of Edward Lear, collected by Holbrook Jackson. Dover, New York.

The Scholastic Rhyming Dictionary, edited by Sue Young. New York: Scholastic, 1994.

Wombat Stew, by Marcia Vaugh. Silver Burdett Press, 1986.

Books for Teachers

Booth, David. *Classroom Voices.* Harcourt Brace Canada, 1994.

Booth, David. *Literacy Techniques.* Pembroke, 1996.

Booth, David, with Bill Moore. *Poems Please.* Pembroke, 1988.

Buzzeo, Toni, with Jane Kurtz. *Terrific Connections with Authors, Illustrators and Storytellers: Real Space and Virtual Links.* Libraries Unlimited, 1999.

Close, Susan, with Faye Brownlie and Linda Wingren. *Reaching For Higher Thought, Reading Writing Thinking Strategies.* Arnold, 1988.

Close, Susan. Tomorrow's Classroom Today, Strategies for Creating Active Readers, Writers *and Thinkers.* Pembroke, 1990.

Esbensen, Barbara Juster. *A Celebration of Bees, Helping Children to Write Poetry.* Henry Holt, New York. Can only be ordered from: tory@ttinet.com or 612-929-2065.

Fox, Mem. *Radical Reflections: Passionate Opinions on Teaching, Learning and Living.* Harcourt, Brace, 1993.

Freeman, Marcia S. *Building a Writing Community*. Gainesville, FL: Maupin House, 1997.

Goforth, Frances S. *Literature & The Learner*. Wadsworth, 1998.

Hodges, John C., with Mary E. Whitten. Canada: *Harbrace College Handbook*, HBJ, 1986.

Jobe, Ron, with Mary Dayton-Sakari. *Reluctant Readers*. Pembroke, 1999.

Jobe, Ron, with Paula Hart. *Canadian Connections*. Pembroke, 1991.

McCormick Calkins, Lucy. *Lessons from a Child: On the Teaching and Learning of Writing*. Heinemann, 1983.

Moore, William H. *Words That Taste Good*. Pembroke.

Nodelman, Perry. *The Pleasures of Children's Literature*. Longman, 1992.

Papert, Seymour. *The Connected Family, Bridging the Digital Generation Gap,* Atlanta: Longstreet Press.

Spink, John. *Children As Readers*. London: Clive Bingley, 1989.

Books for Kids about Writing

Aliki. *How A Book Is Made*. Harper Trophy.

Bradford, Karleen. *Write Now!* Scholastic.

Bower Ingram, Anne. *Making a Picture Book.* Methuen, Australia.

Christelow, Eileen. *What Do Authors Do?* New York: Clarion Books.

Ellis, Sarah. *Young Writer's Companion*. Groundwood, 1999.

Gunnery, Sylvia. *Just Write!* Canada: Pembroke.

Stevens, Janet. *From Pictures to Words, A Book about Making a Book.* New York: HolidayHouse.

Stinson, Kathy. *Writing Picture Books*. Canada: Pembroke.

Stinson, Kathy. *Writing Your Best Picture Book Ever.* Canada: Pembroke.

Teitel Rubins, Diane. S*cholastic's A+ Guide to Good Writing*. New York: Scholastic.

Index

Virtual Maniac—Silly and Serious Poems for Kids
Margriet Ruurs
For students in grades 3-8

Here's a book of poetry for every day and every reason. Margriet Ruurs' poem-stories describe familiar feelings, like those you have when you look at shapes in clouds or feel the fall. Readers meet funny characters like Bruce, the almost-always fearless dog; the boy who just can't story playing video games; and silly Anna-Belle Lou, who turns her hair blue. **$7.95**

The Writing Menu
Melissa Forney
For teachers of grades K-5

Tired of trying to teach writing to students who have different learning styles, interests, and attention spans? One "writing size" doesn't fit all! The Writing Menu offers an innovative alternative that nurtures success in every student with a cafeteria-style menu of prompt choices for expository and narrative writing across the curriculum. Includes grade-appropriate target skills. A variety of genres, projects, and topics validates student choice within a solid, standards-based structure. **$14.95**

Non-Fiction Writing Strategies
Marcia S. Freeman
For teachers of grades K-5

Enhance the quality and effectiveness of your school-wide writing program with a balance of expository writing that integrates science with writing! Here's how to use Newbridge Early Science Big Books as models of good writing to teach the information-writing techniques so critical for student success on performance-based writing tests. Includes strategies for teaching writing-craft fundamentals, step-by-step explanations of the basic process of teaching writing-craft skills; oral and written models; student examples, practice activities, and assessment procedures; a variety of expository techniques, with related precursor activities appropriate for the youngest writers; advice to prepare your young writers for success on performance-based tests. **$19.95**

Building a Writing Community—A Practical Guide
Marcia S. Freeman
For teachers of developing writers, K-8

New and experienced teachers of developing writers in grades K-8 appreciate this comprehensive and easy-to-use resource that helps create and maintain an effective writing workshop. Over 350 "What Works" and a practical approach help you teach young writers style and genre characteristics, composing skills, conventions, and the many aspects of the writing process itself. Elementary schools love the very useful fold-out skills development chart included as a bonus. **$23.95**

Teaching Writing Skills with Children's Literature
Connie Dierking and Susan McElveen
For teachers of K-5

Twenty well known children's books become models to teach expository and narrative writing skills in this innovative and very useful resource. Students learn about brainstorming, focus, organization, elaboration, and writing conventions with readily available children's literature. Using the techniques of good writers as models, the authors take you step by step through each component of the writing workshop mini-lesson. A primary and intermediate level lesson for each selection make it easy to match the mini-lesson with the readiness levels of students. Selections are especially chosen to illustrate target skills. **$19.95**

The Bookbag of the Bag Ladies' Best—Resources, Ideas, and Hands-on Activities for the K-5 Classroom
Karen Simmons and Cindy Guinn
For teachers of grades K-5

Ever wanted to put together a really fabulous thematic unit —but you didn't know where to begin? Start here and add hands-on pizzazz to your thematic units! These teachers use everyday items like cereal boxes, newspapers, and CD cases as props for easy, classroom-proven projects that encourage interactive learning and motivate K-5 classes. Step-by-step directions, drawings, black line masters, and photographs for 48 projects—all you need to build thematic units geared to your own curriculum. **$19.95**

1-800-524-0634 • www.maupinhouse.com